Also by Jane Holman

Pearls of Wisdom: For Your Path to Peace

Seeds of Self-Care: For Love and Serenity

Light

Ignited

Miracles

Unleashed

A Cosmic Blueprint for Your Miracles

LIGHT

IGNITED

MIRACLES

UNLEASHED

Jane Holman

the kind press

Cover design by Miladinka Milic
Editing by Tegan Lyon
Internal design by Nicola Matthews, Nikki Jane Design
Photo credit: Julia Keep

 A catalogue record for this book is available from the National Library of Australia

ISBN: 978-0-6455237-9-9
ISBN: 978-0-6455237-4-4 eBook

For Zoe,
Your love and light awakened mine.

Miracles that arise in the outer world are birthed within.

CONTENTS

PART 1
Miracles Ignition:
Magic and Miracles Panacea

PART 2
Messages from the Mystics: Gods, Goddesses and Otherworldly Beings

PART 3
Emerging Abilities

DEAREST MIRACLE WORKER

Thank you for showing up and believing in your deep knowing, a knowing that tells you that infinitely more and magically more is possible. Your great intuitive inner power is urging you to realise that you are capable of substantially more than life has revealed to you and for you... yet. Oh, how it is brewing, can you feel your own potential desiring to burst forth to create a life beyond your wildest imaginings?

I say 'beyond' because to be in a state of miracle manifestation, we need to go beyond ourselves. If we keep doing and being the same, much of the same shows up for us. Each time we ignite more light within, we awaken and activate our miracle personas and power. As you become deeply immersed in the energy and messages of this book, you will come to know that miracles that arise in the outer world are created within.

This book is about taking your light beyond where it has ever gone before, deep into the heart of your miracles. I invite you to come on a journey with me beyond your current self to your ignited self.

YOUR
MIRACLES

You have opened this book; you have opened the door to your miracles. I define miracles as extraordinary, often inexplicable, most-welcome events that appear to be divinely orchestrated, and I also paradoxically perceive miracles as typically 'ordinary' events. Miracles often can't be explained, only perceived, and sometimes open us to more questions than answers. Miracles are open to interpretation. What I consider extraordinary may be deemed ordinary or even pass by completely unnoticed by another. Miracles in my world are also unexpected moments of joy, deep love, profound gratitude and innate peace. To me, unplanned, surprising pleasure of any kind is a miracle. Anything that brings me healing on an emotional, physical, or spiritual level is a miracle. Epiphanies and deepening awareness and consciousness are also miracles in my miracle playbook. In fact, anything that lights us up at any moment could be considered a miracle.

If you had a personal definition of miracles, change it or expand it in some way to allow it to encompass more than your original definition. With miracles (as with most responses to life) it all comes down to perception and points of view. Exponentialise your baseline for miracles. Witness and notice your miracles to invite your miracle persona to come into existence, perhaps slowly at first, and then in a more profound, even prolific way. Observing and acknowledging miracles has an uncanny way of drawing them towards us with greater speed.

All miracles are miraculous, and all are possible.

Allow miracles to join you and your life in small increments to begin the journey into the world of miracles. Eventually, you may also find that as you flex your miracle muscle through desire, intent and expectation, miracles can also be monumental occurrences that facilitate great transformation and change. When we step into our super selves, functioning from love, power, belief and alignment—with co-creation as our natural state of being—we are magnets for miracles.

Something is stirring within you, changes are brewing, and you are getting free of those long-held conditioned and ancestral patterns that limit you. The past and all of your old patterns are shaking loose. You are passing through the eye of the needle, leaving behind what can no longer fit with the next evolution of you. This requires bravery, trust and belief in our process and worth as we gently move through discomfort (as things rise to heal and release). You are now stepping into being the conscious awareness behind your mind and you are ready to see what you are truly capable of—and so is the world that you orbit. One person stepping into their miracle personas creates a ripple effect—a cascading of miracles—and we become miraculous beings living on a miraculous planet.

Remember, your living is your miracle.
Your experience of life will show you exactly what
needs to go, along with what you need to open up
to in order to receive all of you, that is, the miracle
worker you came here to be.

✳

IGNITING YOUR LIGHT

'There is a light radiating from within you,
that glows with all the strength, grace and
courage you need to grow forward.'

- Adele Basheer

Anything dark within can be shifted and transformed by receiving your light. When I refer to inner darkness, I am talking about anything within that allows strong unpleasant emotions or thought patterns to remain unprocessed and therefore stored within, limiting all that you can be and experience.

Continually asking, 'What light can I shine on this?' brings in the energy and awareness of what you need to let go of, that is, anything that is obscuring your inner light and inner love. It is already within you waiting to be the dominant force.

If you have read my first book, *Pearls of Wisdom: For Your Path to Peace*, you will be aware of the deep inner work required to get out from under your turmoil and identify the honest work required to connect to the truth of you and your wisdom, awareness, peace and potential. You have learned that finding your wisdom through all that life presents and, more importantly, your reaction to each experience leads to your peace. If you have read my other book *Seeds of Self-Care: For Love and Serenity*, you will understand the power of self-care to connect with your love. You have learnt to take care of yourself by responding to life in such a way that it becomes self-care. You consistently seek connection with wonder, awe, love and the vast array of elevated emotions that are invoked by prioritising wellbeing through self-care.

PUTTING YOUR MIRACLES INTO MOTION

Our miracles can't be rushed. They occur in Kairos or divine timing, most likely when we are ready for them and are showing up for them through our strong self-love and self-worth. Feeling good and powerful helps to manifest our miracles because they are more readily drawn to us. Being in alignment with our higher selves and universal flow is most conducive to miracles. Avoid placing emphasis on what is not working in your life as it is not a 'miraculous' use of energy. Focus instead on all successes—both tiny and monumental.

Remember to continually review and expand your definitions of a miracle. Any change, any new awareness, and any freedom from a pattern or addictive tendency is a miracle. The high-vibe energy that you radiate is a miracle. Excitement, enthusiasm and inspiration are all miracles.

Proactively activate your miracles. Expect miracles: make a demand, say often, 'Universe, show me a miracle!'. We need to bring forth our greatest belief, commitment and determination to be in the space for receiving miracles.

Never underestimate your confidence, loving presence and all the great attributes you possess as your miraculous power. This power is felt by all; utilise it well.

You've done the work, you are amazing, not only to yourself but also to others. You are finally willing to see and be the miracle of you. Now what? Now it's time to play: to use your god or goddess powers; to be the miracle that you are; to create, to manifest, to inspire, to turn your light onto full ignition. You came here to activate your stardust and shine. It may be a gentle twinkle or an expansive, cosmic night sky. We are all one and any light has the potential to ignite the light in others.

What will you choose?
Where will you go?
How will you heal?
How will you inspire?
Who will you be?
How will you serve?
What will you create?
How will you lead?
Who will teach you?
Who will you connect with?
How will love express itself through you and for you?
Where is your magic?
Where are your miracles?

———————————————

Coincidences and synchronicity are central to universe's way of making miracles. Don't miss your miracles, they desire to be witnessed so we can ignite them even more.

———————————————

PART 1

Miracles Ignition:
Magic & Miracles Panacea

We are all beings of light; igniting our light is the
essence of our miracles.

We each have our own unique entry points to miracles.
Each person has several keys (portals) held within for
unlocking miracles. Our life-path and our ensuing self-
awareness guides us towards turning these keys. Our keys
are sacred. My willingness to identify and turn my own
sacred keys allowed me to move into the space of receiving
and creating miracles. It became possible to engage a
miraculous force that forged ahead in my life, paving the
way for all that I required and desired (for my highest
good) to land when I needed assistance most.

Miracles come alive through our heart space. Connect
with your heart space, the seat of your power and the
connection to your soul as often as you can. When I
connect with my heart space, I like to think of something
beautiful. I picture an unfolding rose emanating white
light, swirling rainbow colours or stars. Develop your own
symbol to remind you to connect with your heart. You
may even like to picture the image on the front cover of
this book for opening your heart space, igniting your light
and opening up to your cosmic potential.

My hope is that this section of the book will open you to your personal blueprint for miracles, unlocking the great unfolding mystery of you. I wish for you to discover the mystical, magical being that you truly are and use this awakening to ignite all that your light encompasses. This will be a doorway to your miracles.

As with my previous books, you may like to read this book cover to cover, highlighting things that move you or that you would like to revisit for further reflection. Alternatively, you may like to use the book as an oracle: asking for the insight you most need to receive today so that you can step into the space of your miracles. Each day is a chance for a new beginning, and you can be brand new each day. Consequently, you may be guided to create a new question before opening the book as an oracle on any given day or moment, depending on what you are currently processing or stepping into being.

The Ignition Tips are for the purpose of providing you with a quick tool for reflection, tuning into the essence of each message and taking some action towards igniting more of your light.

The Illuminative Journalling Inquiry questions are for assisting you to shine a light on what is inside you waiting to be revealed. The prompts are designed to further support you in unlocking the great depths and ancient wisdom residing inside you just waiting for release.

Before responding to a journalling prompt, take a few deep breaths and calm your mind and centre yourself so you can move into your heart space. Make this a sacred time, just for you. You have permission. Write the prompt on a fresh open page, ask to connect with your highest guidance and begin writing. Avoid stopping and analysing what you've written, just let the words flow. You can reflect after the writing when everything that wants to come through for you is on the page. Often, the language that you receive in automatic writing may vary from the language used by you in your everyday writing. Guidance from your spiritual support team and your highest self is generally slightly different to our normal language, or it may be the same—both are great. There is no right or wrong in this process. Enjoy your insight and your increasing light!

Included under each 'panacea' is an 'I am' statement. 'I am' statements speak directly to our hearts and connect us with source energy. These statements will help take you into the space of receiving the deep teachings of each message.

Ask for Gifts, Magic and Miracles

I am worthy of receiving all manner of miracles.

We live in an 'ask and receive' universe. However, we often forget to do the initial asking and at the same time deny ourselves the receiving. Make asking for miracles, magics and gifts a part of your daily living. Incorporate this approach to life, today. Through your asking, you are giving a clear message to the universe that you are ready to receive. Avoid feelings of guilt around asking, and avoid deciding that you are being greedy or asking for too much when you already have so much. Slivers of doubt or lack of belief in our miraculous potential void miracles. Our deep desires and their associated energy (or lack of) radiate into the universe as a powerful form of communication. The universe has radar-like ears, no thought or emotion goes unheard or unfelt. Ask for your gifts from a place of receptive gratitude. Thank the universe in advance for providing for your needs to be met (for your highest good) and for gifting to you that which is beyond your wildest dreams. Be mindful of asking out of desperation, ego dominance or control because these are low-vibe states that will push miracles away from us.

The universe is abundant and unlimited in what it can gift to us: it is a creative force and thrives on creation. Bring the universe joy by giving it something new to work on to draw into existence. In doing so, you are being a miracle worker and expanding the capacity of the universe to create. All of life is intertwined. Creation at its best is co-creation.

For the next few weeks (or forever, depending on what feels right for you as a starting point) ask for gifts each day. After each asking, centre in your heart, in your love, and deeply believe that you are worthy of your gift. Say 'thank you, thank you, thank you' after each request. The universe loves gratitude.

Dearest universe, please bring me something or someone that will enhance my health.

Dearest universe, what gift can you deliver for me today?

Dearest universe, what surprises can I receive today that will light me up?

Dearest universe, what kindness can I receive this day?

Dearest universe, please open the door for me to a new opportunity.

Dearest universe, please send me a sign that your support is near.

Dearest universe, please send me a sign that I am heading in the right direction with this project.

Dearest universe, what more can I learn about myself that I've been unwilling or unable to see?

Dearest universe, please reveal to me a book that will help me grow in awareness, power, peace, and potential.

Dearest universe, please send me a mentor for expanding my consciousness.

Dearest universe, what can I receive this day that will enhance my life?

Dearest universe, what new self-care experience can you place in my awareness for nurturing me?

Remember, all signs, coincidences and synchronistic events are miracles designed just for you. What you have put out into the world has been returned to you with interest, love and kindness for all your efforts. Notice and receive these miraculous occurrences with gratitude and awe.

MY IGNITION TIP

Keep a journal to record what gifts you request from the universe and the accompanying way in which you received the gift.

ILLUMINATIVE JOURNALLING INQUIRY

Where am I over-giving in my life to the detriment of allowing myself to receive?

Awaken From the Dream

I am awakening to the truth of me and to all of life.

Awaken from the dream. Remember your sacred contract. You are more than your earthly persona. Don't be an imposter in your own life—remember who you truly are. Let go of who you've always been as defined by others so you can evolve into your authentic, unique greatness—your miracle persona.

When we arrive on Earth, we have forgotten our true nature, our connection with love, and our divine purpose and mission. Soon our wisdom calls and we receive little nudges, 'aha' moments or even epiphanies. Life becomes about remembering, thereby removing the veils of illusion that keep us from being all that we are (divine miracles).

Love is the path for awakening. *Seeds of Self-Care: For Love and Serenity* will show you the way if you've been a little lost from your love. Each time we connect with love we move closer to seeing the truth of ourselves and all of life. Fear keeps us hidden from our true potential, purpose and greatest light.

To awaken to ourselves and to step into the space of miracles, we undertake a great journey of unlearning everything we thought was real, finding that it most likely wasn't very real at all. Most of what we believe has often been embedded in us at a very young age: learned via the thoughts, feelings and reactions of significant others around us. Once we begin the unlearning process, we are awakening from a deep sleep, no longer trapped in a never-ending dream of illusion that was woven by others.

As we awaken, we learn to question and discover our own truths and innate wisdom. This state of questioning unlocks so much more of us. We become open to receiving universal guidance. Awakening allows us to be free of the majority, we no longer conform and follow blindly; we now see. We listen to quiet wisdom and are no longer coerced by dominance, manipulation and control. Imagine an awakened world. The possibilities are infinite. Miracles would become the new normal.

To awaken means we accept and appreciate discomfort as a guide while we look within to clean up and clear what limits us. We pave the way for the peace and potential we desire and require for our greatest living. Awakening means we give up resisting stepping into the greatness of who we truly are, whatever that may feel like and look like. We welcome change, newness and transformation. We appreciate that awakening can be a messy, challenging, non-linear journey with many highs and lows and much revisitation of old lessons to be fully free and awake to the truth of ourselves and our potential.

Once we've awakened from the dream of separation and our falsely learned reality, we learn to hear our inner voice, our intuition. Once we tune into and hear our innate wisdom, we become miracle makers because we can now hear the whispers of the universe. We are awake; we remember we are spiritual beings having an earthly experience and we access our full potential and power, fully activating our divine missions and soul purposes.

Awakened, we are now open to love, the abundance of all that lights us up, and miracles of all kinds. We can remember our sacred contracts and connect with the guidance that moves us forward on our journey back home to ourselves. **Our sacred contracts are miracles in and of themselves.** We know deeply that we are more than our previously learned earthly personas. Awaken to all that is truly you. Unleash the full spectrum of your light and potential. Your life and love will thank you for it.

MY IGNITION TIP

Release yourself from the definitions of you that have been defined by others. You no longer need validation from anything or anyone else outside of you. Be willing to see the truth of you and life will further show you the way to receive all of you, for you. Create yourself anew with each step towards awakening. Enjoy getting to know you. Trust that the awakened you is beyond amazing.

ILLUMINATIVE JOURNALLING INQUIRY

Dear guidance team,
What is my sacred contract?
What am I being called to remember?
What do I need to be free of to fully awaken?
What greatness do I need to see within me?

Be a Leader in
Your Life

I am the leader of my life.

Be a leader in your life. Lead with love and light. Conscious leaders create miracles often just through their presence and an inherent power for stimulating transformation. Our energy, when we are willing to lead, can cause miracles—transmuting many low vibrational states into higher vibrational states. You can lead your family, your colleagues, your friends and, on a larger scale various movements and organisations, if you feel so inclined. It is okay to be seen, to go first, to pioneer new approaches and thinking. Give yourself permission to shine, to step beyond your 'normal' to your extraordinary. Being a leader means you are helping others to step up purely by your example. Leaders create environments conducive to inspiration and the birth of miracles. Leading can positively impact individuals and yourself at the same time. Through leadership, you are truly serving as you are honouring life and your responsibilities within it. In this space, just being all of you encourages miracles.

The work that you do on yourself can create miracles for others. Your awareness can shine light on the things those around you are processing. You get to be a mirror for others. The work you are doing on yourself (around processing and integrating your emotions and beliefs) is paving the way for others to do the same. You are leading by example. You are walking your talk. The best teachers are the best learners. Leading and learning inspires us, ignites our light and elevates our vibration to generate and receive miracles.

MY IGNITION TIP

Find what inspires you and lights you up to the degree that you must share this with others. Your energy of leadership will elevate everyone into the space of potential miracles.

ILLUMINATIVE JOURNALLING INQUIRY

Where am I being called to step up and lead, where previously I have chosen to follow?

Becoming Unlimited

I am unlimited, and my miraculous life is unlimited.

Miracles are generated when we are willing to become the unlimited energy of what we desire to call into our world:

- If we desire success, we need to feel successful already.
- If we desire to receive in a greater way, we must know we are worthy of gifts.
- If we desire deep love and respect from others, we need to develop great self-love.
- If we wish to create miracles, we have to be willing to receive miracles.

We have not (as yet) learned how to be unlimited as we have no reference point for our infinite potential. We need to be willing to go beyond what we've always been. Making the conscious choice to be unlimited (even when we don't know what that is) opens the door to our new space of unlimited beingness and unlimited miracles. The universe will take us by the hand and guide us in baby steps and even large incremental leaps, towards a life that we may previously have considered out of reach for us. Intentions are everything when making the choice to release limitations from our lives. Becoming unlimited requires opening one's mind to infinite possibilities. It requires a commitment to exploring all that may be possible for us. Freedom from limitation requires total belief in you, your desires and your dreams.

Choosing to become unlimited invites the energy of miracles into our lives.

You will know you are stepping into your unlimited persona when:

- The time of your manifestation power is enhanced, that is, the gap between your desires and their arrival in your reality shrinks.
- You experience moments of, 'Wow, I didn't see that coming.'
- You develop talents and abilities that had been previously dormant within you.
- You become deeply interested in the cosmos and your possible star origins and connections as your consciousness has expanded beyond Earthly life.
- You are granted total creative freedom in your current line of work, or life in general.
- You experience many firsts because you are stepping beyond your current reality into new realms.
- You embrace the unknown and are amazed by what appears.
- Your life unfolds effortlessly with increasing joy and expansiveness.
- You are in a regular state of wonder and awe.
- You seem to be doing less but are actually attracting more.
- You find that you are spending more and more time doing what you love.
- You become keenly interested in the mystical and magical.

- You move away from control and into a love of flow, spontaneity and surprise.
- Time expands for you. You can achieve much in a limited timeframe.
- You often have moments of deep gratitude, often saying to yourself, 'How did I get so lucky?!'
- You live in a state of, 'What else is possible?'

Being unlimited means we have access to all of the infinite cosmic potential.

MY IGNITION TIP

Be infinite, take your awareness out into the universe. Expand out into the universe for millions of kilometres in all directions. What might you find calling out to you that is beyond your wildest dreams?

ILLUMINATIVE JOURNALLING INQUIRY

I am unlimited and what will I choose next?

Believe Deeply

*I am a divine creator of
miracle-inducing beliefs.*

Miracles arise out of faith and faith begins with our beliefs. I wish someone had taught me in my childhood or in previous decades that my beliefs can change (if not create) my life. I would have encouraged my beliefs to work towards my miracles far earlier than I did. However, what has stunned me in the most beautiful way is how truly miraculous it is to change our beliefs. In fact, in my experience, things generally change within days or weeks of changing my beliefs. That is how amazingly powerful we are! **We draw evidence of our beliefs towards us.** Our lives reflect our beliefs.

*'What you believe has more power than what you dream
or wish or hope for. You become what you believe.'*
- Oprah Winfrey

Do your beliefs need a makeover, a re-vamp or an update?

Your unconscious beliefs (about you and life in general) directly impact your life experience and how others perceive and relate to you. Work on gently uplevelling your beliefs to support and reflect all that you desire and require from a place of kindness and compassion, not from a place of self-judgement. Make peace with your beliefs; there is nothing wrong with you for having them and they have got you to where you are today: ready for more. We are all perfectly imperfect. If we were perfect, there would be little room to grow and change. Once awareness is brought to unconscious beliefs, wisdom, power and freedom flow into that space.

To allow more of you to show up, seek to understand why your beliefs are in existence. Free them to become something new, something that may serve you and your life far better. Compassionately accept your beliefs, see them truthfully and then consciously choose what your next steps may be to uplevel them, just for you.

Understand how your beliefs either empower or disempower you.

The hurt, wounded and traumatised parts of our minds will always 'knock', attempting to take us away from empowering thoughts and possible future great beliefs. Refuse to answer this call. Breathe in, breathe out and release limiting thoughts: you really don't need them anymore because your new way of being and living is drawing closer. You are a living miracle, so you get to be in charge. Make your beliefs and feelings your miracle magnets: they are what you radiate out into the world and simultaneously draw towards you in like. Anticipate a big life. Believe that your miracle has already been delivered... and your wishes granted.

Our thoughts are the secret sauce for changing how we feel and for directing what shows up in our life. Keep thinking the thoughts that most deeply align with how you want to feel and what you'd like to create until they are fully integrated within you to the point that they become new beliefs. Changing our beliefs is miraculous, but it is no easy feat and requires focus and commitment. The great news is that it becomes easier, especially as you get to enjoy seeing how things begin to change within and in your outside world. Every increment of change in your beliefs is worth celebrating. Every time you catch a thought and re-direct it towards a better feeling thought, you become a step closer to establishing beliefs that are more worthy of you and where you desire to lead your life. Moving forward is miraculous and makes us feel good— further consolidating the power and potential of our belief work.

Create momentum in your life by getting off the 'to and fro' thoughts dilemma, that is, the constant split between positive thoughts and the counteractive and limiting, momentum-depleting thoughts. Miracles can arise when your thoughts are directed for your good, all the time. This is when you will truly know your power and potential. Consistently align your thoughts with your greatest desires so you can enter the space of miracles.

It is natural that fear will re-surface during all stages of belief work. Remember, our egos are disconcerted by change and will try to convince us to maintain a familiar status quo. In this instance, our rising fear is indicative of change. Be patient with yourself, as is the requirement for all transition stages. Gently change your fear every day, one thought at a time to build a greater belief and trust in the unfolding of your beautifully designed life. **Fear limits the goodness we can feel and the greatness we can radiate.** Loosen fear's grip to connect more fully with your purpose, allowing you to share your gifts. Showing up for our new beliefs and corresponding talents and abilities rather than resisting them (through fear) shifts unease and anxiety and allows for greater peace and miracle momentum.

Find the truth under any limiting beliefs, get honest with yourself and determine what the reward is for keeping limiting beliefs in place. Do they allow you to keep playing small, stay safe, and hide and avoid showing up as the leader or teacher you know you can be? Do you get to play the victim or have an excuse for not moving or changing? There is nothing wrong with any of these choices, but they don't generally provide fertile soil for miracles to flourish.

Keep believing and telling yourself the stories of how you desire your life to be; delete the limited versions so you can rewrite the greatest story of your life. You have nothing to lose other than what no longer serves you. The elevated version of life that is awaiting you is your greatest gain. Keep your eyes open to witness the ripple effects of change that are beginning to occur through your commitment to aligning your beliefs with what you desire to invoke.

Feel how you want to feel in advance of your beliefs reshaping your life; this will give them greater wind in their sails. Trust deeply that everything you are working towards is also working its way to you in the best possible form for your highest good. The magical thing is that we can change our beliefs in a heartbeat. We can choose new ones that help us co-create all that we desire and require. Our thoughts and beliefs influence our vibration which is the creative force behind all we draw into our existence. Our nature is to seek growth and expansion, and managing our beliefs is the first step towards being and receiving more. Approach changing your beliefs from a place of compassion, from the rightness of you, never from the energy of wrongness. Your beliefs so far have helped you create what you've established in your reality at this moment in time. Honour your process and the relinquishing of old beliefs for expansive new ones.

Acknowledge small steps and each piece of evidence that your belief change work is starting to bring great newness to your feelings and life. Deep trust is essential even if the seeds planted have not yet bloomed. Doing belief work allows us to step even more into our power and creativity. Believe to receive.

What do you do when your thoughts and concurrently forming beliefs are not supporting the next version of you and the life that you desire to invoke?

Sit in your current mood and your current state and be honest with why you are feeling how you are feeling. Take out your journal and ask, 'What is the message, the truth under what I'm thinking and feeling right now?' What am I resisting stepping into? Who am I avoiding being? What am I avoiding doing? Where have I knocked myself down by going into comparison or judgement?

Move your mood up the emotional scale by one thought and action at a time. This may require meditation, movement, connecting with your oracle cards, immersing yourself in nature, ocean time, bathing, retail therapy or whatever form of self-care, nurturance or pleasure is going to elevate your mood one increment at a time. Be compassionate with yourself. Don't expect to move from despair, grief or any other low-vibe state towards joy in a single heartbeat. Most of us require gradual processing of our emotions and self-coaching or assistance from others to step into a better space. It is hard to feel good until the thinking has been re-routed to support feel-good emotions. Start in your current state—which is the perfect place to begin. Remember, mood is everything in providing the foundation for encouraging thoughts and their associated beliefs to arrive and thrive.

Be vigilant, even when all is well and strong belief is evident. Negative ego-based thoughts can infiltrate even the most powerful minds. Without airtime, less-than-favourable lines of thinking can't take root. They are weeds, don't water them. Your new beliefs are too important to allow sabotage to negate them. Our lives change when our beliefs are consistent and empowering over long periods of time. It is your choice how you use your mind and what you choose to think and believe, but always know you have the power within.

'Taking responsibility for your beliefs and judgements gives you the power to change them.'

\- Byron Katie

MY IGNITION TIP

Play around with belief change work today—
don't leave it another second. I know you
will be pleasantly surprised with what transpires.
Establish the most healthy, supportive and
life-enhancing beliefs so that you can trust
yourself above all else. Create a list of beliefs that
will support you and your work. Commit to reading
them daily until they are integrated with your psyche.

ILLUMINATIVE JOURNALLING INQUIRY

We can change our future by changing our thoughts and associated beliefs. What evidence of changing beliefs does future you desire to experience?

Be Open for Miracles

*I am open at all times to
miracles for my highest good.*

Many of us desire miracles on one level and refuse them on another. Refusing is evident when we make excuses for why we can't do or receive certain things. When we start using 'What if this happens?' statements to avoid trying something new or changing a pattern, we inadvertently shut the door to our potential miracles. Recognising that these excuses are just the ego's attempt to keep us safe (and limited) helps to diffuse the impact. The ego's voice quietens over time as we practise trusting and backing ourselves and our choices. Refusing to play small allows for large miracles as we move away from ego functioning and into higher-self functioning. Intention is everything.

Akin to excuses is resistance, that is, blocking our forward movement and suppressing our miracles. We may procrastinate and say to ourselves 'we should do this before we can act' or completely avoid taking steps towards new miracles, expertly distracting ourselves with something else. Resistance is tricky to navigate because sometimes it can be our awareness encouraging us to slow down and take some extra steps. Feel into your body and tune into your heart to know the difference. This will help you feel the truth.

Be open to new opportunities. Adopt the 'Universe, I am open for business' attitude to create doorways for miracles. The universe is unlimited and says 'yes' to our desires, but we are the ones who say 'no' with our energy, unsupportive beliefs and negative thinking. Eradicate settling for second best. You are worthy of your first and best choice or desire. Removing settling from your repertoire indicates that you are worthy of so much more and gives your soul permission to call in what you truly desire.

Stay open in order to receive intuitive guidance. Guidance is always available to lead us along the path of miracles if we are willing to be still, tune in and listen. I act according to my intuitive hunches, pulls and calls so I am in the best position to receive miracles that may be circling. Observe and witness what is occurring for you with great presence and acknowledgement.

Be alert and ready for synchronistic events so you can be in the right place at the right time to see, hear, feel or experience something that may be required to receive your miracle. Expect miracles to receive miracles.

Be relaxed about what may or may not happen. As soon as we become vested in outcomes, we slip into control and force (often unsuccessfully), thereby pushing miracles away from us. Flowing with and surrendering to what eventuates is a much greater use of our power. Act and then retreat; allow the universe to orchestrate how your miracles shall be presented to achieve your highest good.

Be patient and confident. Neediness or any type of victim story or sense of entitlement draws our miracles away from us.

Raise the frequency of your surroundings to open your space and invite in beautiful miracles. Miracles are drawn to beauty and love of all kinds. Flowers, candles, great feng shui, cleanliness and uncluttered, aesthetically pleasing environments are conducive to high vibration and miracles. Clear your space of lower energies by burning sage and letting in fresh air and sunshine. Bless every space you enter with light and love.

MY IGNITION TIP

If your interest is piqued, say yes to what life presents. You can always choose again when something no longer lights you up. Saying yes indicates our willingness to embrace a big miracle-filled life. We need to try many things to fully appreciate what makes our hearts sing. A singing heart is a harbinger of miracles.

ILLUMINATIVE JOURNALLING INQUIRY

What baby step can you take today towards a new opportunity or experience that is calling?

Be Willing to Be Too Much

I am all that I am and beyond.

Be willing to be too much of all that you truly are—no more hiding or boxing up parts of you to conform. Be your own version of too much.

Too fun.
Too rich.
Too powerful.
Too beautiful.
Too free.
Too kind.
Too successful.
Too emotional.
Too ambitious.
Too smart.
Too aware.
Too funny.
Too weird.
Too different.
Too wise.
Too loving.
Too enthusiastic.
Too optimistic.
Too excited.
Too sensitive.
Too abundant.
Too extraordinary.

Sit with this list and tune into where you may have decided too much is just too much for you or those around you.

We limit our miracles by limiting ourselves because they ultimately arise from within. We attract what we are so give yourself permission to be the most magnificent version of you, whatever you discover that to be! In other words, be willing to be the true authentic expression of yourself no matter how much that may impact those around you. So often we close down too much of our presence in an attempt to make others feel comfortable around us so they are less jealous, less intimidated and less whatever-it-is-for them so that we feel liked, accepted and comfortable. In doing this we shut down much of our exuberance and our enthusiastic excitement for life. Live through the most childlike, lit-up version of you to power up your potential for miracles.

Celebrate your 'too muchness' and let it expand even more. Honour yourself by embracing and sharing all of you.

MY IGNITION TIP

Be radiantly too much. Power up your life force
to be a force: a force to be reckoned with; a force
of nature; a force for miracles.

ILLUMINATIVE JOURNALLING INQUIRY

Complete your own 'I am' list. Boldly declare all of your talents, abilities and attributes: all of the places where you may have been considered too much. Own it all.

Brain Breaks

*I am the awareness and the
manager of my mind.*

I regularly talk with clients about taking 'brain breaks' to reset their thought patterns to receive wisdom from their higher self as opposed to listening to the ego. Brain breaks are times when we speak directly to the ego, saying 'NO' to any rabbit hole it wants to take us down. Take control of that thing, insist it is quiet when you require it to be. Challenge yourself to have times without random thinking, processing and stories on repeat. You will know you need a brain break when your thinking becomes negative, worrisome, or repetitive—playing the same script or dramatisation on repeat and causing uneasiness. Brain breaks are required for inner peace and access to our wisdom and intuition. The radio dial is tuned to the wrong frequency when plugged into the ego. The higher-self frequency is where the magic and miracles arise. To induce miracles, we need to live from the space of our higher selves as our ego functioning does not beckon miracles. Our ego keeps our miracles at bay because it does not like change, growth, new possibilities or entering the unknown, all of which are requirements of being open to magic and miracles.

Taking brain breaks allows us to take charge of our minds. We become aware of when it goes off on its own tangent, attempting to channel us into worry, dramatisation and over-processing, constant analysis and making up stories to keep us limited. We must quieten this part of our minds if we wish to activate our miracle minds (higher self) and miracle selves. Our potential, awareness, insight and creative imagining arise through our higher self when the ego is quiet. It requires great training for the ego to be quiet.

Changing up our daily routine in any way circumvents the ego functioning to a great degree. The ego likes familiar patterns and routines as it is easier to lock us into the same repetitive daily thinking and corresponding emotions. This is why when we take breaks from our home and change our environment and routines we often see changes in our thinking and emotions. New environments and routines often bring new awareness and inspiration. We require lots of reset experiences to distract the ego from its habitual programming. If you can't change your scenery regularly, at least vary the structure of your day. This might mean having breakfast, exercising, meditating, checking messages, travelling to work, lunchtime routines and after-work routines occurring in different ways and at different times—all will serve to distract the ego from its normal mode of repetitive control.

You will know you are functioning from the higher self when messages and thoughts coming through for you are positive, based on intuition and awareness, and are even inspirational in nature. You will begin to enjoy mentally quiet times as the ego will be diluted with the higher self at the forefront, always willing to help you activate your miracles. You are now the awareness and manager of your mind. Life is about to change since your mind can now be used to create miracles.

MY IGNITION TIP

Catch your thinking in the moment you know that you are no longer the 'awareness' programming its direction. Take charge of your mind by re-directing it and determining what exactly you desire to think about in any moment. Remember the power of your thoughts to create your life. Our thoughts radiate out into the universe and will serve your miracles more effectively if they come from the higher self as opposed to a fearful, out-of-control ego.

ILLUMINATIVE JOURNALLING INQUIRY

What practises still my mind and allow for higher-self contemplation and intuition?

Reading, Reiki, exercise, nature-time, meditation, yoga, automatic journal reflection and water calms my mind. What works for you?

Collaboration

*I am a great partner in all
of life and I collaborate and
elevate through love.*

When clear intentions are combined with elevated intent
and emotions in a group setting, potential and possibility
increase exponentially. The powerful combination of like-
minded souls coming together for a purpose can create
miracles: think resonance and the synchronous vibration
of something nearby. Inspiration, intent and wisdom
in this sense can also resonate and increase in strength.
Resonance could be likened to dropping a pebble in a pond
or, on a larger scale, the tsunami effect of earthquakes. We
can become tsunamis of consciousness and miracles when
we combine our power, love and wisdom with others
towards a higher purpose.

We as human beings with powerful energy fields are
connected in ways we cannot even begin to perceive. Many
believe in the power of combined prayer to bring about
change. Large collaborative group experiences where
individual after individual is raising his or her vibration
means that the entire group can operate at a higher
frequency. Higher en masse vibration is transformative,
healing, uplifting, inspiring, alchemising and miracle-
inducing. Come together with beautiful like-minded souls
for a higher purpose and explore what else is possible
for you, others and humankind in general. Embrace the
infinite possibilities of miracle contagion. Start a miracle
circle. Sharing miracles with others makes miraculous

energy contagious. There is great power in groups of high vibrational beings coming together with purpose and meaning.

MY IGNITION TIP

When you look forward to seeing a colleague and feel light and inspired around them—when your soul sees and connects with theirs—there is potential for the power of collaboration.

ILLUMINATIVE JOURNALLING INQUIRY

What would opening to collaboration look like, feel like and be like for me right now?

Connect With Your Future Self

I am forming a loving connection and clear communication with my future self.

One of the most powerful things I have trained myself to do is connect with my future self to create a greater life experience today. I first heard about this practice decades ago but didn't really connect with it until recent years when my level of belief was ready to actualise and sustain it.

Maybe I had made the connection at a soul level, if not at the mind level, as the life I'm living now would have been beyond my wildest dreams back then. I remember Gary, the conference facilitator asking us to connect with our future life and draw it into the now to speed up the process of our greatest evolution. Once again, belief is everything and all-powerful in undertaking 'future self' work. When engaging with your future self, you are showing ultimate trust in yourself, your journey, and the amazing future you are designing and crafting for yourself. He or she has already paved the way for you. She's done the work; she's accessed your wisdom and universal wisdom and applied it with great success. Celebrate and thank you in advance for all that you have been, cleared, levelled up and transformed on the journey to becoming all of you, super you, miracle you.

Connect with future you through whatever means are conveyed to you on any given day. I find oracle cards, journalling and meditation great practices for connecting with my future wiser, more enlightened self. You can ask: 'What would my future self like me to know?' before doing these activities. You can also be specific, asking for information pertaining to the dynamics of your relationship, business, career path, current self-care needs or general health and wellbeing.

Connecting with your future self today:

Through meditation, you can take your body and soul, hand on heart to the place in the future where you are healed and whole.

You can take yourself into the future to a place of great happiness and draw this towards you.

Take yourself into the future to a time of the highest vibration and draw that into the now.

Move to where your future self is at their most wealthy and abundant and draw that towards you.

Go to the future where you have met your great life partner and draw those feelings of love towards you.

Travel to a time in the future when you experience great success and draw that energy to you.

Take yourself to the place in your future where you have your ideal health and fitness and draw that knowledge and vibe towards you.

My Sample Future Illuminative Journalling Inquiry:

What would my future self like me to know that would enhance my life, today?

All is well. This book is already published and well-received. You are just going to love and be lit up by the beautiful cover design. Feedback for your transformative text will bring you much joy. Just keep showing up for the writing with trust, belief and love in your heart. See this book as a mystery unfolding. Much of the content from here on in will be revealed to you when the time is ripe for it. See each part as a new juicy piece of fruit ripening at the right time, ready to be picked. The mystics, goddesses and otherworldly beings of light will reveal themselves and their words (for the world) to you as they see fit for their place and time in this transformative work. Your beautiful trilogy is a gift to the world. Honour and celebrate you and your work every step of the way.

What can my future self reveal to me about the upcoming content that is required to be shared with my readers?

Dear Jane,

The content will become even more surprising, exciting, and intriguing for you as you connect even more deeply with your own miracle persona. The miracles that are circling around you, readying to land in your reality, will further fuel your passion for the words that are revealed by you and through you. It will be your most exciting living and writing space to date. You will lead, inspire and write by example. Your light will draw even more mystics into your orbit, ready to contribute to this beautiful body of work. Enjoy this unfolding.

MY IGNITION TIP

It's time to meet with your future self. Trust that future-you is wise beyond measure, happy beyond measure, successful beyond measure and miraculous beyond measure, with much to pass onto you to draw your best life closer to you, today.

ILLUMINATIVE JOURNALLING INQUIRY

What would my future self like me to know right now that will enhance my life today?

Create the Space
for Your Miracles

*I am potential arising
out of stillness.*

Miracles are seeded in the potential of stillness. Embrace your moments of quiet. Regularly practise moving from the pace of life to the peace—the calm of it. Quiet times create the space for miracles to glide in, often unexpectedly and unannounced. In quietness, miracles can be witnessed. Miracles that are noticed are so powerful that they themselves open the space for drawing in more miracles. Miracles often have a snowball effect. We are excited by them, love them and therefore send the signal out into the universe that we are ready for more of them. We move into the zone of miracles. Love attracts love; miracles attract miracles. We also invoke the power of gratitude to further fuel our miracles as we respond with joy and wonder to the miracles we have created.

Oftentimes we are too busy or too distracted to notice and receive miracles. Miracles occur with greater frequency and with the magic of synchronicity when we have the expectation for them and have created the possibility of them with our peaceful, most powerful selves. Controlling, forcing and rushing at a frenetic pace of life subsequently pushes them away as these states lower our receptive vibration.

Make seeking opportunities for stillness and quiet reflection integral aspects of every day. Quietly connecting with your higher self through any form of meditation, movement or time in nature are great ingredients for miraculous moments. Our light is ignited when we are peaceful and content as we are most connected to the wisdom and potential within us waiting to be accessed.

Create space to receive the new miracles by letting go of the old. Miracles like a void. We don't want decades of unnecessary junk blocking the path of our miracles. They are lined up everywhere waiting for us to be clear enough to receive them.

A change of scenery provides a great reset, setting us up for miracles. When changing our environment, we are distracted from ourselves and our usual repetitive thought patterns and emotions, providing space for newness— which is another form of miracles. Any change is a miracle as many of us love our comfort zone. When we create ourselves anew, we create our lives anew—and that is miraculous.

The unlimited unknown is the birthplace of miracles. We generally only create from what we know, so stepping into the unknown opens us to greater possibilities. We move out of certainty and control into flow and potential. Expanding our consciousness, raising our vibration, and stepping outside of our current reality and into higher dimensional states and frequencies is the idyllic space for miracles... miracles beyond our wildest dreams because we created the space for them.

MY IGNITION TIP

Regularly step back from the busyness and predictability of life. When possible, take yourself to previously unknown places to re-set so you are ready to receive the arrival of the new potential awaiting the space. Be prepared to enter the unknown where infinite possibility exists.

ILLUMINATIVE JOURNALLING INQUIRY

Where is my unknown? Where do I need to go? What do I need to experience to open more space for miracles in my life?

Feel Miraculous

I am love and I feel love.

The fastest route to drawing in miracles is to feel amazing. How you feel will be your barometer for indicating how close you are to being in the space to create miracles. Miracles exist at high-frequency levels. We need to raise our vibration to meet them. When we feel good our vibration is high. Follow your joy for it will lead you to your miracles. Elevate your emotions one moment, one thought and one action at a time to change your energy to invite in miracles. **Make the commitment to move away from what does not feel good, including your own thinking, after you have processed what needs to be cleared.** Being happy places us on the same frequency as success, abundance and miracles of all forms. Rise up.

To feel good, you must take care of yourself as if you are the most precious child in the universe. My second book, *Seeds of Self-Care: For Love and Serenity* will show you the way if you are feeling a little undernourished in the self-care department. Replenish your life force to be the force behind your miracles because everything arises from within you.

As your high vibrational state draws miracles to you, your cup must be full to create the space for miracles. If your cup is emptied, the miracles may possibly be drawn to someone else whose cup is brimming over. Miracles are drawn to love; your over-flowing, fully replenished cup is magnetic for miracles.

Another important component of feeling miraculous is to live your life from the space of silver linings. Find your silver linings as they are there in abundance, you may just need to look for them from a greater, higher vantage point to fully appreciate them. Adopt the stance of living as if all of life, the challenges and the problems all have silver linings: things to learn for transformative growth and detours to place you in the right situation and mindset to receive miracles curated for you. There is always a positive to every perceived negative if you are willing to open yourself to greater awareness and new perspectives. Living from the space of silver linings helps us to cultivate optimism: as one door closes several more are flung open.

To feel miraculous, we can also train ourselves to flow with all of life as opposed to resisting what is occurring. This involves trusting that everything is unfolding for our highest good, even if in the short-term things are feeling unfavourably tough.

Regardless of what is happening, it is important to keep our hearts open. Difficult experiences can often lead us to a place of erecting protective walls. Unfortunately, our armour can also keep out all the great things that desire to come our way. Balance your need to protect yourself with allowing in love in all its shades.

Nature gets a mention in all of my books, it is impossible for her not to; there is still so much we can learn and connect with through our experience of the natural world. Spend time in nature to anchor yourself into feeling miraculous. Ground into her.

Merge with the miraculous nature vibes all around you: tune into the vibration of the birds or the bees, they will remind you of your desired frequency. Nature creates miracles from moment to moment. Be in awe of these miracles to cultivate your own miracle persona. We must remember our connection to nature and allow her energy to flow through our bodies. Many cultures hold the belief that giving back to nature, even in small ways like planting a tree or weeding a garden, magnifies our manifestation process. Caring for nature brings us good fortune. Many believe we also enlist the assistance of the elementals when we actively support nature.

Give yourself permission to feel good without sabotage and an endpoint. I learned this lesson the hard way. I had been having an out-of-this-world magical day. I felt phenomenal, my energy was high, and I was so excited by the events that were unfolding moment to moment throughout the day. I felt like superwoman... but then slowly creeping in from that tiny ego voice was, 'This is just too good to be true, can this really just keep going, there must be an endpoint.' Part of me had decided that I had received way too much goodness in one day and I, therefore, manifested an endpoint, a minor tripping over, fall to the ground in dress, knee-grazing moment that was enough to rocket me away from the land of miracles where I was currently residing.

Miracles arise from expansive, limit-free emotions.
Believe in infinite greatness, possibility and self-worth-
fuelled deservedness.

My Ignition Tip

Believe that your very existence is all that is required to birth miracles. Know in your heart that creating miracles is easy and comes naturally to you and that there never has to be an endpoint for them for any reason, ever. A coherent heart and mind both working in harmony to bring about your miracles is very powerful. Make sure your life provides a strong platform from which to launch your miracles through your unwavering commitment to feeling miraculous.

Illuminative Journalling Inquiry

What would you have to choose or change today to feel amazing and attract your miracles?

Freedom Day

*I am free to be an imperfectly
perfect, authentic me.*

One of the greatest gifts we can give ourselves is freedom from perfectionism. Make today your Freedom Day. It is a choice. Needing to be perfect limits our miracle manifesting power as we spend inordinate amounts of time putting off creating anew because we have decided things are not yet perfect enough for us to act. Life becomes a waiting game. We wait to seek a particular experience or relationship or career opportunity until we are slim enough, or fashionable enough, or clever enough, or rich enough, or popular enough, or smart enough, etc. We all have our own versions of 'barriers' we erect to limit our progression. We are not here to be perfect. We are here to grow, learn, try new things, heal, become aware, teach, find out what we are truly capable of, to love and be loved and step into the unknown (our place of miracles) as often as possible. Being okay with being less than perfect (and even judged) gifts us the miracle of showing up as our authentic selves and then the real miracles designed especially for us can begin.

Granting ourselves Freedom Day challenges many aspects of our persona that we may not have previously questioned. We may now give up not being willing to be 'too seen or too heard,' in effect coming out of hiding. We may release the need to constantly please others at the expense of our own needs. We may reach for our dreams, minus all the usual reasons why we cannot act to bring them to fruition. We may see ourselves with loving eyes now that perfectionism is no longer our chief way of operating. We may allow our light to be our guiding force, choosing what makes us happy rather than perfect.

We can't ignite our light and unleash our miracles if we are too afraid to put a foot wrong or make a mistake. We cage and even extinguish our light and any potential for miracles if we are frozen by our need to be perfect.

MY IGNITION TIP

Invite love into your life to help shift perfectionism and its associated shame for not being enough, doing enough or having enough. Re-ignite the light that may have been dimmed through fearful, judgemental responses about your worthiness.

ILLUMINATIVE JOURNALLING INQUIRY

Where am I enough in ways that I have been unwilling or unable to see?

Imagine and Envision

I am a visionary, and my imagination expands my creativity daily.

Everything that exists and will exist in the future was seeded first in someone's imagination. Our miracles exist on the other side of our imagination. What are you willing to envision into your reality or even further afield, into a new world reality? Create a beautiful bond with what you are imagining. Love it into existence. Many dreamers can weave a greater new reality for the collective.

Intuitive hunches arise when we are elevated in our vibration via our imagination, leading our creative process. Our imagination is a platform for envisioning our miracles. Allow yourself to dream big, to hope, to be inspired, to be ignited by your passion, to act when guided and do so via your intuitive powers, and to put your beautiful manifesting miracles power into motion. At the same time, focus on the journey, the process, the learning, the unlearning, how you feel and what you experience along the way. The destination is very seldom what we expect it to be. If we stay away from focussing on success (you're already successful in any moment and in any situation, it's just a point of view) and enjoy what is presently unfolding, surprise and miracles can arise out of the infinite unknown. We close 'infinity' when we require immediate results of a pre-determined nature. Be unlimited by staying open to possibilities. Certainty is rarely a space in which miracles can arise with ease. Always maintain the space for the unfolding of more with a 'what else is possible for me and my life?' approach to day-to-day living.

Our dreams are only limited by our imagination. Fantasise, get creative and allow the universe to take your dreams beyond what you ever thought was possible. Allow your dreams to be interwoven with miracles. Trust in your visions before they become a reality. Imagination requires us to embrace the unknown and to allow life to be an unfolding magical mystery.

Just for this chapter, I'm going to invent my own word: 'imaginate'. The reason for this is that our imagination is an integral part of creation. We create through our imagination so please 'imaginate' often. Our imagination is all-powerful. Remember back to childhood... it was how we lived, it was how we felt our world, it was how we expressed ourselves, it was how we sourced our joy, it was how we drew all that we were envisioning into our world. Our task is to reconnect with the child-like versions of ourselves who were willing to fall into the beautiful world of our own imaginations; from here we have the opportunity to bring our dreams to life.

Miracles are seeded in the imagination.

- Allow your imagination to move to the forefront of your being.
- Allow your imagination to be unrestrained and unlimited.
- Allow your imagination to show you your hidden desires, dreams and predispositions.

- Allow your imagination to excite you, inspire you, awaken your dormant dreams and their accompanying talents and abilities.

If you can imagine it, you will draw in what is required to create it, such is the power of you. Be excited, be elevated via the portal of your unlimited imagination. Imagine and envision. Imagine and envision. You have permission. Use your imagination to heal you, to take you to previously unencountered places and situations. Your mind won't know the difference and your body and life will reap all the benefits of the power of your miracle-filled imagination. Unleash your miracles via your imagination. Dream it and be it: 'Imaginate'.

MY IGNITION TIP

Meditation is a great way to explore and develop
our imagination. There is nothing to do but
'imaginate'. Believe in your dreams as most will
believe in limitations, yours included.

Avoid allowing the energy of small-minded
individuals to infiltrate your beliefs and dreams.
We need your miracles, and they arise from your
belief system.

Surround yourself with the supporters, not the
naysayers, as they have forgotten how to dream
and can't help you. Many around you have chosen
a safe and small life of limitation. Show them that
unlimited is possible. Break all the rules of your
current reality; birth your dreams with the greatest
of ease and in the perfect way for you—in a way
that is beyond your wildest dreams.

ILLUMINATIVE
JOURNALLING INQUIRY

Where can I go in my imagination that will take
me to new places and creative spaces?

Know That Peace is Your Birthright

I am peace, and peace is my power.

I continually emphasise the importance of peace and love as precursors for miracles. In my first book, *Pearls of Wisdom: For Your Path to Peace*, you are guided towards uncovering your own wisdom for creating (your) peace through all that life presents: developing awareness and new wisdom around life's major themes, highs and lows, and adversity. You will come to appreciate that your life has been an 'expert' in helping you to be revealed, for you.

Make peace your priority because when you are peaceful, you are your most loving and powerful. Know that you deserve to live with inner peace. We cannot control the outside world, but we are responsible for our inner world and our inner peace. Work consistently on establishing a beautiful inner life. This will come naturally once you have undergone the process of shedding all that is in the way of your peace, requiring much unlearning of what you may previously have known to be true, often originating in childhood. If patterns and beliefs stemming from our childhoods are not brought to light for our new adult awareness to review, they can shape and even define our future. We weren't taught as children that we oversee our own destiny and that our lives are created by our very own beingness: our thoughts, feeling, emotions and beliefs.

Become your own source of comfort. Trust that anything can change, and anything can be healed if it is for your highest good. Know that you are never alone. Your guides, light beings and angels (or your version of higher guidance) are with you all the way, often showing up in the form of animals, insects, books, talks and teachers—letting you know through signs and new insight that they are with you. Your spiritual team will always help to guide you back to peace if you are open to listening and observing.

Peace is maintained more readily when we know that we are not our thoughts, and we are not our emotions. Ask yourself when you're feeling something that does not feel light for you, 'Is this really true for me?' Perhaps it is just an old, conditioned belief, something that you adopted from a significant other at an impressionable time in your life. Be truthful with yourself. Being totally honest with ourselves will eventually set us free to be all we can be and consequently assist us to receive our own miracles. **When we are honest and stand in our truth, our consciousness aligns with and reflects our reality.** In this space, peace and truth combine to create our miracles. Our 'truth' changes daily alongside our reality. Sometimes grief is our truth if we have experienced loss. We need to honour our emotions, feel them and accept them, so we can move back to peace sooner rather than later. Know that peace is your true miraculous nature, regardless of what life presents. We are powerful enough to feel sadness or to experience suffering but also to feel peace at the same time. We can place all that is not peace in a small compartment to deal with, without letting it infuse our entire being with lower vibrations. Our truth, combined with love, transmutes much of what comes between us and our peace. Life is an ongoing spiritual practice, embrace it all. Our souls know that our suffering gives birth to our greatness, our higher selves do not fear adversity only we do in our human selves. Find your peace in that pearl of wisdom.

MY IGNITION TIP

Breathe in the truth that from your peace all other great emotions can arise. Be grateful for all that brings you peace as inner peace raises your vibration to an ignition point for miracles. At the same time, have gratitude for all that does not bring you peace as this will challenge you enough to crack you open to receive your own wisdom, light and potential for miracles. Breathe in and allow your life to be as it is and breathe out resistance to everything that is. There is great peace in this.

ILLUMINATIVE JOURNALLING INQUIRY

What do I need to clear within to feel whole, to feel peace?

Know Thyself
and Life

*I am aware of all of life and my
place and purpose within it.*

To be miracle workers, we want to show up as our best selves, for us and for life. Life on Earth is not always easy and often downright challenging. Awareness and functioning are everything.

> *'The degree to which a person can grow is directly
> proportional to the amount of truth they can
> accept about [themselves].'*
> - Leland Val Van De Wall

We want to know, understand and have compassion for ourselves (the whole truth), and at the same time, know and understand life and our place and purpose in it. All things are connected, so understanding us (and life outside of us) simultaneously contributes to our miracles.

Miracles are grown through knowing life and being one with life, making us more powerful as we connect to love from a place of greater peace and understanding. We need to move our focus towards establishing connection and oneness rather than separation. To enhance oneness, become acutely aware of when and how you go to judgement as that is how we separate from others and life itself. Empathy on the other hand creates connection.

'The highest form of knowledge is empathy, for it requires us to suspend our egos and live in another's world.'

- Plato

Peace within and peace in life is the ultimate life-changing endgame; it is miraculous, and it comes from knowing ourselves and understanding life and our place within it. We long for meaning and an understanding of our place within life. A part of knowing thyself is also about knowing when to forget thyself. Sometimes forgetting ourselves and gifting all our attention to another distracts us from useless concerns and moves us away from ego functioning. Service helps us to connect with others and life while still developing personal awareness. Serving well involves serving us well, ultimately providing the greatest foundation for our service.

One must avoid the path of many spiritual advocates, that is, becoming too focused, too absorbed in self. Balance is key: having a healthy understanding of self, one's shadow aspects and the healing required is essential for being most effective in life, and for experiencing and receiving all of life without resistance or adverse reaction. It is equally important to have awareness of the human condition and where we are both limited and moving forward as a collective. Miracles arise from awareness and understanding. Knowledge is power.

MY IGNITION TIP

Care for yourself by taking a break from thinking
about yourself. Set yourself free to just be.
So much of our days can be spent worrying
about ourselves and our place in life. Take a holiday
from it all, it isn't supportive of us to be working
on ourselves all day every day—we don't work at any
'job' non-stop around-the-clock. Be peace, let it be,
let it go, even just for today. Be okay with all the
ebbs, flows, cycles and seasons within you, in all of
life, without needing to process it all the time.

ILLUMINATIVE JOURNALLING INQUIRY

What can I let go of to relax into being me today?
What is the collective experiencing right now
that is also true for me?

My Work is My Life, My Life is My Work

*I am living, being and creating
my best work.*

When our best living becomes our best work, we feel wholeness and contentment beyond compare. We love life on a whole new level when we love our work. Our work lights us up from within and then powers our best living. Miracles arise out of loving our work and our life as we radiate high-frequency energy. We are in service to ourselves and to life. When we serve life, life serves us in return.

When in love with our life's work, we are more likely to be aligned with our deepest beliefs, desires and soul purpose. We trust in what is unfolding for us and this trust becomes our platform for opening to and generating more. Each day is a new day filled with aliveness and a constant feeling of 'what else is possible for me, my life, and my work?' When inspired in this way, we step into cutting-edge creativity. With a stance of infinite possibility, we instantly connect with our inner miracle maker, knowing exactly what is required for our next right action.

Intent and purpose connect us with our higher self: our all-knowing and our all-loving essence. As we take one step forward to more greatness, the universe often has a miraculous way of taking many more steps on our behalf, fully supporting that which is for our highest good. The universe responds to positive intent and action. We become miraculous and unstoppable with the universe rallying alongside us.

Connecting with our deep purpose inspires us profusely, placing us in great love. Love creates movement, it transforms and is unlimited in its potential and possibility. The more I love my work, the more it loves me. I am in awe as I am open to so much more: more light, more potential and more connection with the mysterious and magical power of the unknown. Miracles arise from the unknown elements of life. We are miracles waiting to happen, moment to moment. Feel your purpose, feel your dreams, feel your desires: feel them in your heart, mind and soul to activate their true power. Open to more, for you are more. **Work your light to fully ignite your light.**

Living and loving your work with balance is the key to success and optimal well-being. We still require some healthy boundaries between work and play (no matter how much we live and breathe our work) to maintain our equilibrium and equanimity. This is especially easy for me when I'm on holiday away from home. I am still working when I feel inspired to do so, however, there are more opportunities for self-care with no home responsibilities calling. Stepping away from our work often has the effect of increasing our motivation, gifting us a new perspective, magical insights and new inspiration.

I am sure time expands when we are doing what we love. When you are lit up from your work you will make miracles happen. Steps that ordinarily may need to be taken will be bypassed. You will do less and attract more with greater ease and satisfaction. Your energy will expand, igniting those around you to step up into their own space of creative genius. Your creativity will be heightened beyond measure, and you will feel free and powerful. Your ideas will come to life in the most miraculous and surprising ways.

Find what you enjoy doing or are especially good at and turn it into paid work. Connect with what you loved doing as a child to find clues to lead you to work you will love. As a child, I loved books and reading. I would create libraries of books and 'professionally' lend them out to friends and neighbours. I absolutely treasured stationery and would collect beautiful writing implements and paper sets. I loved my typewriter and would type away for hours.

Look for the potential in all that you have loved in your past or dream about now as an avenue to explore possible work options. Your intuition will always lead you to where you need to be to love what you do. Be patient because often it takes a long time for the stars to align and our dream work to arrive. Enjoy your unfolding process because it is just as important as any destination and is in fact great preparation for what is to come.

My journey saw me working in clothing boutiques and then establishing a long teaching career which was also great preparation for observing and writing about life. I also did an editing course because I thought I might like to become an editor. The writing was obviously calling but I had not heard it at this stage. Next, I put to work decades of interest in alternative therapies by establishing an energy healing and intuitive coaching business before embarking on my writing journey as an author. The work with clients inspired my interest in transformational literature. Each step led me closer to the work of my heart—my destiny work. Looking back, I can see how so much of this initial work was preparing me for now.

For me, living and working are completely intertwined. Every moment of every day I am open to insight and writing inspiration. This could be whilst enjoying a cup of tea in the sunshine or taking a bath. If I'm not working on my 'work', I'm working on me. While on vacations away from home I am extremely connected to my work: ideas might flow in on the plane or whilst out on the water or after meeting new people. Work filters into everything I'm doing and being, and I love it that way. Even when working with clients, it is like spending time with like-minded friends (such a gift) who I can be myself with. I love the privilege of being a small part of clients' beautifully unfolding journeys through life. I no longer require 'holidays' from work, because wherever I am, I love what I do. I can work from anywhere, such is the flexible nature of being a writer.

The more we show up for the work, the more
the work shows up for us.
The more we show up for our miracles, the more our
miracles show up for us.

MY IGNITION TIP

Look back on your own journey to find revealing patterns and potential insight as to where life may be calling you to new purpose and new work.

ILLUMINATIVE
JOURNALLING INQUIRY

What did I love experiencing and creating as a child?
What do I love doing in my current life that I could
turn into paid work?

No Time to Die

I am alive and open to all possibilities for my best living.

Life on Earth is a gift, the most precious jewel. However, there is a caveat: it is a life we get to hold onto for only a short, fleeting time, especially if we relate it to the infinite expanse of universal time.

Live your life from the space of, 'your last breath may be tomorrow' and see what you create with that highly fuelled motivation for living. There is nothing to lose but everything to experience. Feel the freedom that comes from living with abandon. No part of you is held back and life is there for the taking. A life of miracles cannot be lived from the sidelines. Immerse yourself in all of life; jump feet first into the unfolding adventure that is your life. Say yes to life, to every opportunity, to every possibility. Release the mundane and embrace the extraordinary. Treasure your time on Earth as the miracle it truly is. Receive the opportunity your life presents to create miracles of all kinds.

Some viewpoints to embrace for making each day count:
All that I need for this lifetime has been within me all along.
There is no time to waste before I die.
There is much to create in this life.
I will be everything I came here to be.

I leave no desire unexplored.
I show up for all my gifts, talents and abilities and allow
these unique attributes to bring me my best life.
I live courageously and beautifully and then I get to die
exceptionally well.
My last breath will be a sigh of contentment for all that I
have been and all that I have created.
I leave behind a legacy of miracles on Earth no matter
how long I 'chose' to be here.
Every life is a miracle, regardless of time.

My Ignition Tip

Have all your desired creations in existence
before you die so you can reflect on your life
with pride in who you were and what you achieved.
Bring forth your miracles today, there is no
time to waste.

Illuminative Journalling Inquiry

What legacy do I wish to leave behind on Earth?
What steps do I need to take today to bring my
creations to life?

Open to Guidance

*I am an open and clear
channel for guidance of the
highest good.*

Opening to guidance from our higher selves and
spiritual team is life-changing and miracle-inducing.
Guidance is a miracle. We no longer have to feel alone
or unsupported. We always have access to our team. Our
guides await our call any time, day or night. They are patient
and kind and always have our highest good at the centre
of all communication. Connecting with our guidance
moves us into the greatest version of ourselves, assisting
us to draw forth our calling, and that is miraculous. We
remember our true nature as spiritual beings having an
earthly experience. We are on a journey back to our best
selves and we are calling in assistance of the highest calibre
to align us with the greatest version of ourselves.

To connect with our guidance the first step is to open
our hearts and minds to such a possibility. We need to be
open in order to receive insight. It is a free-will universe.
We have a choice at any moment as to what we allow into
our world.

Next, we need to tune into the way that we receive
communication and signs. This experience will be
influenced by our predominant clairs. For example, if you
are clairvoyant, you may see images in your mind's eye. If
you are clairaudient, music may speak to you, or you may
hear insight in your own voice. Many individuals receive
guidance through dreams, meditation, oracle cards and

automatic writing. Many connect with guidance while in nature or when immersed in water.

The key is to trust the guidance that comes through for you. We each have our own unique codes to analyse, along with a natural approach to receiving information. Spirit will tune into your preferred way of receiving signs and information. Many people see repetitive numbers or images of things that are special to them: butterflies, rainbows, birds, white feathers and so on. You can ask for a particular sign to become a personal symbol for you to indicate when you are on track and another symbol for showing that a different pathway may be beneficial. When your guidance team knows you are committed to this experience, the signs will become more prevalent and personal to you. Your guidance team knows you best and will continue to develop more specialised means of communicating with you. The style of communication will change as you evolve and develop greater awareness and gifts for connecting with the spiritual realm. If you take one step, the universe will take ten more on your behalf. The universe rewards intent and effort.

Your guidance is fuelled by action. As your connection to universal guidance (guides, angels, loved ones, ancestors, source, gods, goddesses, mystics, nature and so on) grows you will become more adept at asking for guidance, listening to your intuition, decoding signs and symbols, and acting on this information accordingly.

Avoid allowing doubt to negate your guidance; believe that what you see, hear, smell or feel is purposeful and real. Learn the language of love that the universe uses to communicate with you, for you. This experience will bring you great comfort and peace. You will begin to trust yourself and back your choices, decisions, awareness and actions.

My experience of communication is a combination of many elements and I imagine this is the case for you too. Generally, I see an image or symbol in my head, with my third eye. The symbol or image comes in very quickly and then forms colour. The images are often formed around my life experience; there is a frame of reference that I can relate to and connect with. Next, I will hear words to accompany the image, deepening clarity. Often a feeling or a knowing (an extension of the information) will also drop in. Most often a knowing or intuitive hit will circumvent everything and there will be no need for words or images. My 'knowing' can often be accompanied by tingles, goosebumps and changes in body temperature. I often also see sparks of light in my peripheral vision. When channelling with clients, the experience and imagery can change as I'm also connecting with my client's guidance team which is such an amazing experience and I always feel blessed, honoured and appreciative. Often I will see clapping hands, stars, a compass, wheels and rainbows signifying growth, alignment, celebration and blessings.

We have a divine right to tap into our own insightful light and make a connection with the universe.

We were born with these abilities but taught (often inadvertently) to forget them and not believe in them. It is an innate part of who we are and it's time to remember it.

My Ignition Tip

The fact that we can receive guidance from our higher self and guidance team is a miracle that fuels further miracles. Believe in the guidance that is coming through for you. Use it to draw in your best miracle-filled life: healing you and energetically enhancing those around you. Allow your guidance to give you a higher perspective around you and all of life.

Illuminative Journalling Inquiry

In what ways does my guidance team connect with me?
How can I open my channels of communication with my spiritual team?
What do I need to release to better hear the voice of my higher self?

Pass to the Future

*I am always connected to the
best time and space for my
greatest progress.*

I have come to know after my share of reactions and dramas in this life that whoever invented the saying, 'this too shall pass' was a wizard of truth.

I now conserve my precious energy by jumping to the future when something with the potential to take its toll on me has occurred. I ask, 'Body, energy, take me to three days from now (or whatever time frame feels appropriate to the scenario) when this energy has passed, released'. Things immediately lighten, significance is removed, and space opens for wisdom and possibility to descend.

We find solutions and insight when we function as our best selves, and sometimes a little distance, a jump into the future, can provide just that. Heavy energy or energy taken for processing our reactions (although vital for our health and wellbeing) does not put us in the immediate space for manifesting and receiving miracles. It is difficult to move forward until we have effectively processed the past. A leap forwards for insight to then take us back to the present moment can be highly beneficial. Dramatic low vibrational reactions push away our hearts' desire, rather than draw them in. We need clear bright energy for opening to our miracles. An attitude of 'this too shall pass' quickly helps to put our miracles into motion as we ascend above the drama to conscious awareness. We become the observer of our reactions and the wisdom underneath attempting to surface, rather than becoming the effect of our emotional responses.

MY IGNITION TIP

Work with past, present and future you in the best way possible to create the strongest foundation for your miracles.

ILLUMINATIVE JOURNALLING INQUIRY

What do I most need to take a break from right now by creating a little future time when this current issue is resolved?

Receive Your Personal Earth Curriculum

I am the star in my life, and I excel at creating miracles.

We are all stars in the making because we all contain stardust and the wisdom of the universe within us. To be a star Earth pupil and a great Earth inhabitant, receive your personal Earth curriculum without resistance. Learn to love all of your earthly education. Be happy with all that is presented on your life stage as it has been designed perfectly for you... yes, all of it, even the experiences you did not enjoy. Within the unpleasant 'escapades' you can perhaps now perceive the power and potential for the creation of your miracles.

An important course that you may choose to sign up for in Earth school involves feeling what you need to feel, to free yourself. Remember, your emotions are teachers. Feel them, face them and release them to become more of the miracle you. Sit with your discomfort; it will show you what is required to free you of limitations delaying your miracle persona from revealing itself to you. Meditation, energy healing, asking for guidance and automatic writing are all great methods of accessing the truth and the wisdom underneath our discomfort.

Gaining awareness of your emotions (and your accompanying reactions) will assist you to emerge on the other side of a great bridge, one that leads to your miracles.

When you graduate from each class you sign up for at Earth school, you make a huge difference... as every person that encounters you or walks passed you is changed by you. You become a walking miracle.

We learn most about ourselves by interacting with life. Life is our teacher. All our relationships show us much of who we are and how we respond to life. All our reactions bring us closer to understanding the truth of us. Life mirrors back all that we see before us. Clearly see all of you and all of life to ignite your light and recognise and create opportunities for miracles.

MY IGNITION TIP

Forgive those who have pushed your buttons the most—for saying what you didn't want to hear. These characters on your life stage have shown up to teach you something about you, something that may set you free of a limiting pattern. Receive the gift.

That comment that incited your anger may have been just what you needed to seek change or to step up in a new way. Those words that invoked your sadness may have increased your determination to seek your joy. Sometimes the tough stuff in life is also the good if we are willing to perceive and receive it.

ILLUMINATIVE
JOURNALLING INQUIRY

What Earth school curriculum course is calling to
me for enrolment so I can move into my next level
of awareness and potential for miracles?

Release Your Curses

I am free of all my curses and transmute them into greatness.

I wonder if it is possible to finally reach a point where we have completely had enough of the way we have always functioned. Can we have clarity around it all and reach a tipping point where we change everything in a heartbeat? I know this can be true and it was an out-of-the-blue miracle of magnitude for me and my life. The universe conspired to beautifully orchestrate what I call, 'Release My Curses Day'. Curses for me are self-imposed, there is never any outside force involved: just powerful me. My curses have arisen when I have chosen to limit myself in any way by my thoughts, beliefs, attitudes, and emotions.

When are you open to receiving your Release from Your Curses Day?

My 'special' moment arrived on a gorgeously sunny day when I was feeling so amazing (every second of the day). There was no low energy, no fear, no worry, no concern, or stress, just a feeling of joy to be alive and sense of great, miraculous possibility. It was relentless and I loved it. However, there was this tiny niggle in the back of my mind that questioned how much longer this could go on for. It felt too good to be true. Somewhere I had doubts that the sweetness of life could be mine all day every day.

Since our thoughts and beliefs create our lives... enter my 'bingle bungle'. All my patterns were about to be revealed to me at once!

Whilst in a chaotic supermarket carpark with my head in the clouds, enjoying my amazing high vibes and my feet not so fully planted on the ground, I felt a dreaded 'bump' and the associated rapid plummet of my energy. I had backed my beautiful car ever so slightly into another woman's car. This 'gift' simultaneously (in a multi-layered experience) showed me where my self-imposed limitations were still containing my freedom, those places I had inadvertently 'cursed' myself. What transpired was this: I went straight to concern for her and her car (luckily there were no marks on her car) then to her reactions or opinion of me, then to judgement of me, to guilt and shame, then to concern for all the reactions and opinions of the bystanders which then triggered dormant childhood fears of doing the wrong thing or getting in trouble. Rapid, crazy and revelatory.

This car bingle experience allowed me to see the devastating effects of perfectionism: a need to do everything perfectly, to never make a mistake, to always please others, to fear the opinions and judgements of others and to protect my self-worth. These are all curses. This was all crazy stuff that I processed for an hour and then I was done! That was enough! I was never going to those places again because I was worth so much more than that. My power surged like never before and I was ready to release all my curses. I am calling them curses because they were things quietly hiding in me that I don't think were ever mine to begin with. They were things I seem to have been born with that were subliminally wired into my emotional DNA, my ancestral patterns and my energy fields. Today was the day they were no longer going to be a part of me or my journey moving forward. I was setting myself free to be and receive the miracle of me.

What are your curses (crying out) to be released for your Liberation Day?

I release the curse of always putting the needs of others above my own.

I release the curse of, 'This is too good to be true.'

I release the curse of taking on the pain of others.

I release the curse of perfectionism.

I release the curse of low self-worth.

I release the curse of seeking the approval of others.

I release the curse of making myself feel less than.

I release the curse of not believing that I can be blissfully happy in all my days.

I release the curse of caring what others think of me.

I release the curse of giving away my own power.

I release the curse of not showing up as the greatness of me.

I release the curse of needing to hide.

I release the curse of not being everything I am.

I release the curse of not accessing my awareness every moment.

I release the curse of not choosing what's best for me.

I release the curse of negating my own desires.

I release the curse of weak boundaries.

I release the curse of not shining unapologetically in an attempt to make others feel better around me.

I release the curse of not loving myself enough.

I release the curse of not speaking my truth.

I release the curse of not trusting others.

I release the curse of trying to fit in.

I release the curse of fearing people and their words and actions.

I release the curse of needing to justify my choices and actions.

I release the curse of not believing in myself.

I release the curse of allowing others to affect how I feel about myself.
I release the curse of long-held fears.
I release the curse of fearing the suffering of others.
I release the curse of believing I can get sick or catch a disease.
I release the curse of carrying ancestral emotional DNA.
I release the curse of cursing myself.

MY IGNITION TIP

We can work on ourselves for decades, but we can also have the greatest miracle of all: our own liberation day. Give yourself the gift of release from your long-held curses. It will change all of your existence, as it did mine.

ILLUMINATIVE JOURNALLING INQUIRY

What self-imposed curses am I releasing today to set me free?

Release Your Erstwhile Self, Finally

*I am free of the past; it
no longer defines me.*

Our miracle-inducing personas are already within us. All we need do is systematically uncover all that is in the way of our best selves: the kindest, most compassionate, most sensual, wisest, creative, most fun and adventurous, and all the other great selves that are waiting to be reborn within us. We are tasked with releasing our former selves— any selves that are limiting us and our authenticity and true potential. Identify all the ways that you engage in limitation and release these patterns. Limitation occurs when we decide that we don't deserve something or someone that is showing up in our lives for our greatest good and best life. Evidence of our limited functioning occurs when we push love away from great relationships, friendships and opportunities by deliberating doing or saying something to negate what is showing up for us. We need to unlearn this behaviour as we will otherwise remain stuck in a cycle of drawing in loving experiences and simultaneously sabotaging their success. We rarely actualise or maintain our miracles when trapped by ourselves in this cycle.

Connect with your past and make the decision to free yourself of the old hurts you no longer need. You've left these wounds open for long enough, it's time to gently heal and release anything standing between you and the miracle creator you are destined to be. Sit quietly and have a chat with your inner child. Let he or she know that you wish to invite miracles into your life and it is now safe to do so as you are free of the past. Support your inner child; use nurturing and encouraging words just as you would with any young child that you love. Coach your inner child back to confidence, self-love, self-worth, peace, contentment, hope and optimism, one day at a time. Let he or she know that they are deserving of miracles and there is no limit to what they can create and receive.

To finally release our erstwhile selves, we engage in an archaeological dig to rediscover our deeply buried golden selves. To successfully chip away all of the old layers of hindrance concealing our miraculous selves are these essential miracle ingredients: self-care to soothe our nervous system, intent, patience, receiving guidance and opening ourselves to support.

Once we set the intent of becoming all that we can be, the universe will conspire to help us every step of the way, placing the right people and experiences along our pathway to assist us to evolve into our most magnificent selves. Embarking on this journey requires fortitude and endurance as the gift of us will be gently unveiled in a way that is most conducive and supportive of the betterment of our selves. Think of a long game of chess. The universe needs to make many moves to orchestrate wins on our behalf. This game also requires much synchronicity: our openness to receiving coincidences and signs; our ability to intuitively connect with guidance; and tapping into our infinite inner knowing. All these actions occur in divine timing—not our timing. Patience becomes a great virtue in the evolution of us. Breathe and receive your patience today. Be present with what is occurring and unfolding just for you, today. What could be more perfect? Hello new you and new life.

ILLUMINATIVE
JOURNALLING INQUIRY

What can I release today that will allow me to
meet brand new, miraculous me?
How does miraculous me show up in this world?

Releasing Sabotage

I am now free of all sabotaging patterns inherited from others, my family and my ancestral line.

One of the kindest and most life-changing gifts we can bestow on ourselves is identifying our points of sabotage and then challenging them. Our places of sabotage can be found just at the point where we have decided we are not worthy of something, we are undeserving, something feels too big for us, we are not successful enough or powerful enough or confident enough—or fill in your personal blank—to meet it. We reach an inner threshold that demands that we are allowed no more than what we are currently experiencing. It is here that we will meet our self-sabotage repertoire. It can be as simple as saying 'no' to an opportunity or to a beautiful new relationship. Oftentimes, it may be more covert with subtle attempts to ruin something that would be great for us to receive. This needs to go if we wish to meet with our miracles. Sabotage and miracles cannot exist side by side. **Meet your potential points of sabotage with awareness, compassion, and love.** Love is the ingredient necessary to dilute sabotage attempts. When the need to sabotage is challenging you most, surround yourself and the experience in love. Invite in love, rather than defaulting to fear. Ask for the origin of the sabotage to be revealed to you for releasing.

Many of us struggle to rise above the opinions we have formed of ourselves, most often shaped in our childhood and influenced by 'significant' others in our lives. I can trace back comments from influential adults that have subconsciously played on my mind for decades until I acknowledged and released them.

Unfortunately, these beliefs about ourselves are often 'inherited' from others and can perpetuate and govern much of what we allow to show up in our lives. Sabotage has taught us to conform, stay small and be safe by fitting in. Identify these patterns and it is amazing how quickly they lose their hold—they are no longer on automatic pilot and there is greater freedom to change them. Move out from under any unconscious programming.

We become free of sabotage attempts when we know that no one, no experience or no object is more worthy than us, so we allow ourselves the gift of receiving. We come to appreciate that no one can ever love us more than we love ourselves. We get free of the things that we know shouldn't be kept within us if we desire to move forward into our miracle personas. We can then release expectations of others and fear of their judgement and begin to have autonomy over our own reality.

When attempting to free yourself of sabotage patterns embrace your self-care. Nourish yourself back to full power. Avoid all that drains your power: negative people, experiences that weaken your nervous system and any form of media that promotes fear and its associated mass conformity. Fill your mind and life with positive exposure, whether that be in the form of people, teachers, social media, books, movies or podcasts. Lighten the load on your recovering nervous system. Trust that what is for you will come to you for your highest good. You can be sabotage-free and create your best life where miracles are the norm.

MY IGNITION TIP

Know yourself and your triggers to find your
sabotage patterns. Observe yourself. I did this
quite successfully (after lots of practise) when
I first met my husband. From the moment I
met him he treated me in ways I had never
experienced before. It was amazing from the start
and every day thereafter, so much so that I came
up against my threshold for receiving. I didn't
trust what was unfolding so beautifully because it
was not like anything I'd encountered: I was not
anxious, on edge or worried, so I thought perhaps
something must be 'wrong'. Thankfully, I moved
through my sabotage attempts and lived more
than happily ever after. It is amazing how we can
judge something that is unfamiliar (no matter
how wonderful it may be) as wrong.

ILLUMINATIVE
JOURNALLING INQUIRY

Where have I reached a threshold regarding
what I am willing to receive?
Where does this pattern come from and what
do I require of myself to release it?

Take Inspired Action

I am inspiration in action.

The universe knows you are a certified miracle worker and is on hand to guide you every step of the way towards the realisation of your dreams and desires. Find your purpose, listen, act and watch your power manifest exponentially.

Listen to your intuitive hunches and follow the breadcrumb trails. Following your guidance allows things to occur with greater ease and flow, taking away the need for force and control which is less conducive to miracles. Acting when guided allows us to take shortcuts and maximise the potential of our energy.

Take inspired action and then rest and repeat. Combine this approach with belief and trust as your dominant overtones for invoking miracles. From here the miracle approach becomes one of doing less (well) to attract more. Being in miraculous flow supports our desires, drawing to us what we require with greater ease and less effort.

Our miracles arise just as much in the resting phase as they do in the action phase. The resting phase is where we can receive the next intuitive hit or inspired download for the next step(s). Our rest time creates the space for us to receive. If we don't provide a void, there is no space for the new to flow in. A void can create a powerful vacuum for so much inspiration to flow in. After we consistently rest and act relentlessly, the universe responds to our commitment and seemingly takes many steps on our behalf, going ahead and taking care of things in advance for us. I know I have whiled away many sunny Sundays in the garden, often thinking I should be inside making the most of the spare time to write, and instead giving into peaceful rest and rejuvenation... only to find the next day the writing just flows in so clearly and effortlessly. When I create a happy calm space, I am always amazed at what flows through me, for you. Our self-care is an essential ingredient for creating our best work and more miracles.

My daughter stepped into this flow recently. She took very inspired and direct action within moments. We arrived in Queensland from Northern Territory (en route to Tasmania) on the exact day she needed us to be there—all unplanned and unknown prior to our arrival. Her army husband was going to be sent outfield for several months and she decided to come back home to live with us in Tasmania. Suffice it to say, we had her packed up in two days and my son miraculously was there to embark on the long road trip home with her and the dogs. Following her intuition, and taking inspired action meant that bookings were available, she had a travelling companion and the whole trip flowed with ease.

MY IGNITION TIP

Rest, rejuvenate, listen, act and repeat. Remember that the restorative, self-care moments are essential in the entire process and not just something we do when we have run out of energy, inspiration and motivation.

ILLUMINATIVE
JOURNALLING INQUIRY

What restores me and my nervous system
for optimal well-being and miraculous
functioning?

The Miracle of Gratitude

*I am in awe of and deeply grateful
for all the wonderful experiences
that show up in my life.*

The energy of gratitude will change you and your life, magnetising your miracles towards you, such is the enormity of its potency. Gratitude is high vibration inducing at its simplest and best. Miracles arise most frequently from our high vibrational states.

When I began tracking my miracles in response to the call to write *Light Ignited, Miracles Unleashed: A Cosmic Blueprint for Your Miracles*, I quickly realised that I was also tracking (simultaneously) my gratitude, leading to both my gratitude and miracles exponentially increasing. This experience invited me to ponder... are gratitude and miracles mutually inclusive, perhaps even the same thing? At the very least, gratitude and miracles are the most supportive and complementary companions.

In any case:

- Gratitude is synonymous with miracles. Gratitude is interwoven with miracles. Gratitude connects us with love: a perfect ingredient for miracles.
- Gratitude implies presence which is in itself a miracle-inducing state as we are most powerful (energetically and emotionally) when we are present. When we are fully present, we are more willing to notice and acknowledge the beautiful things that are occurring within us and for us—a

true miracle.

- Observing and tracking our miracles draws them to us with greater frequency. Gratitude predisposes us to be in the state of receiving. We often then develop the subconscious expectation of receiving what we deeply appreciate. We become naturally inclined towards gratitude and miracles; they become part of who we are and how we are.

Is gratitude a miracle in itself? My answer is yes, as there is a power and intent within us when we seek gratitude as a part of our very being and as our predominant response to life. Gratitude is the doorway to the fullest most loving expression of us and is therefore a great portal to miracles. Being grateful is connecting with love. With gratitude we are honouring something, being present with an occurrence and reflecting on what has brought us wonder, awe, joy, peace or growth. We are in a reverent, receptive state for miracles through our connection to gratitude. Gratitude is sacred. Gratitude for miracles large and small brings forth more.

'Your sense of awe at all the miracles you perceive around you allows you to think, see, and live more of these miraculous occurrences. In contrast, a state of ingratitude stops this infinite flow.'

– Dr Wayne Dyer

MY IGNITION TIP

Gratitude is a way of being and responding
to life that we need to cultivate if we wish to
develop our miracle mindset and persona. As
our level of gratitude increases, miracles increase
as we are more actively tracking gratitude-filled
moments... our miracles. Open yourself to love as
often as you can through the portal of your heart.
With your hand on your heart connect with all
that you currently appreciate in your life. Speak it
aloud. Gratitude raises our vibration to
meet our miracles.

ILLUMINATIVE
JOURNALLING INQUIRY

What am I most grateful for within me? What
am I most grateful for in my life at this time?

The Power
of Words

I am the magic of words.

Words are miracles. It is almost impossible to imagine a world without words. Take a moment to appreciate the monumental miracle of words. Allow the miracle of words to contribute to you and the unfolding miracle that you truly are. Use your words to help others connect to their miraculous higher selves, divine source and innate miraculous natures. Cherish your words. Use each word well to invoke miracles for the betterment of your life. Use your words to elevate yourself and others. Words are self-care, but they aren't if used to berate yourself. Every word spoken or thought has an energy, a vibration. Make your words powerful. Make your words fuel for miracles. Invoke the power of the 'I am presence' (as I have chosen to do on your behalf in the affirmation at the start of each chapter) to activate your miracles.

Words have energy. Words contain wisdom. Words contain joy. Words inspire awareness. Words invoke emotion. Embrace the power of words. Surround yourself with people and texts that create love through the use of words. Honour the sacred within words. Connect with ancient wisdom through words. Learn to express the truth of you, the authentic you, through words. Learn to heal yourself and others through words. Use your words to capture the beauty and miracles that flow into your world. Words bring awareness, change and transformation.

Words are miracles in action.

Be aware of the power of your words when you step into your miracle persona. Our words can become our own personal law, use them well. For example, my daughter (who has a very special relationship with her brother) stated that she wanted to include him in her wedding in some way. As a male, a bridesmaid wasn't her preferred option, and she wasn't sure what would qualify as an important role. A week after we had this conversation, the celebrant called Julia, stating that she needed someone to witness the marriage... and just like that, Nic had his 'important' wedding role.

MY IGNITION TIP

Create some 'I am' statements to practise the power of using your words to create miracles.

ILLUMINATIVE JOURNALLING INQUIRY

Where am I placing limitations on myself and what can show up in my life through the use of my words?

Through the Eye of the Needle

I am transitioning and emerging into the greatness of me.

Any beautiful creation takes a while to evolve into its magnificence. For your light to reach ignition point, there will be some turbulence along the way. So much clearing, releasing, and unlearning of outdated truths (which often weren't ours in the first place) is required for our light to emerge from its hiding place.

There is a degree of safety and trust that we need to feel to share our light with the world. A peaceful nervous system allows us to have the strength and willingness to release our magic and miracles into the world. Our trust increases with practise and belief. Each time we back ourselves and care for ourselves, we learn to deeply trust our journey through life. Self-care is paramount in learning to love ourselves to the place of igniting our light. Our love is our light. My second book, *Seeds of Self-Care: For Love and Serenity* will help you to nurture yourself and respond to life in such a way that it supports you in accessing and expressing your light.

Revealing our light to the world requires that we move through challenges on an emotional and physical level. Throughout my first book, *Pearls of Wisdom: For Your Path to Peace*, we learn to emerge from challenge and adversity into our wisdom, peace, power and potential. Much inner work is required to release our limitations; this is taxing work requiring great self-care to support our nervous system in gently releasing what needs to go and relaxing into our new way of being.

Physically levelling up into our light can be uncomfortable. We can experience anxiety as old energies standing in the way of our light emerge to be released. We can experience strange tingling and vibrations as our bodies are prepared to receive more light. Health issues may re-emerge as previous patterns and problems are being released. We can also experience a type of vibrational flu akin to the early onset of cold or flu symptoms, but nothing eventuates.

To move through this sensation of being forced through the eye of a needle with greater ease (with only what we require making it through), we need to trust in our process, nurture ourselves deeply and release all resistance to what is not coming with us for our next stage, and simultaneously embrace what is coming for us on the other side of this massive transformation. Avoid allowing self-doubt to be a stumbling block or, at its worst, stop you and your miracles in their tracks. Meeting our power is a warrior's journey. The abundant, light-filled 'miracle' way of life waiting on the other side of our upheaval is worth it. The rewards are great and beyond what we perceive are possible. Our light and life continue to evolve in spectacular new ways.

MY IGNITION TIP

Relax fully and deeply into times of tumultuous transition. The more transition stages you move through, the greater is the evidence that you are uplevelling, ready to meet miracles of increasing extraordinariness.

ILLUMINATIVE JOURNALLING INQUIRY

What is right about me (at this time) that I am not getting?
How am I changing what was once a limitation into new potential?

Tracking Miracles

*I am in awe of my miracles, and
I witness and appreciate them as
part of my very being.*

Tracking our miracles is a great way to encourage their propensity. Simply having the intent, the willingness to observe miracles, acknowledge the magic within them and appreciate the power of these wonderful occurrences helps to build their momentum. In this space, we become the invitation for miracles.

What we focus on magnifies and what we are
grateful for rises exponentially.

When you begin your journey into miracles you may wish to have a journal to record all manner of miracles. Track all the seemingly small miracles. A miracle is any moment of light, ease, revelation, transformation, or joy... often unexpected. Miracles arrive in interesting ways, often not first appearing as a miracle if we have been unwilling to see the gift before us.

Below is a small snapshot of my 'mini-miracle' tracking over the last month. There is no timeframe or order of importance. Our definition of miracles is a uniquely personal one and is deeply influenced by our beliefs and by what we are willing to be, see and receive. Remember to start with the seemingly small miracles (they are in fact all large) to build your ability to receive. The more you pay attention to your miracles and have gratitude for them, the more they will grow and align with what you desire and require for your highest good. I hope you will begin to see that your miracles are intertwined with what you love and have faith in. Love is the power behind your miracles.

- Great new adventures.
- A kinesiologist identifying a mineral deficiency that allowed me to grow back my healthy hair and nails.
- Being invited to join a book club.
- Green rosellas joining me for lunch.
- Peace within and peace in life after crisis.
- Starting Instagram after much resistance to it and being willing to put pictures of myself on social media—coming out of hiding.
- Putting up my client session prices after 6 years of no change in prices.
- Having a ladybird land on me in Winter.
- Completing my 'trilogy' in a miraculous time.
- Given a restaurant recommendation in a large city, having no idea where it was and discovering we'd randomly parked out the front of it.
- Leaving my bag in a restaurant and a man noticing and catching up to me to return it.
- Experiencing out-of-this-world energies in my sleep.
- Elevating compliments.
- Knowing the word count two months before finishing this book.
- The amazing cover designer of this book somehow took the vision I had in my mind and put it onto paper with pure ease.
- New people and experiences to love.

- Mystics showing up to contribute to this book and gaining my attention in miraculous ways: one goddess even somehow managed to 'record' a television program featuring her life. I asked all family members if anyone had recorded this program, and no one had! A miraculous mystery!
- Many beings who wanted to communicate with me dropped 'signs' of their name on objects, images, books, social media, in music and programs.
- New psychic gifts revealing themselves to me, for me and for my clients.
- Surprise invites to events.
- Selling things for double the price even when they weren't initially for sale.
- Beautiful feedback on books.
- Books reaching surprising places.
- A run of amazing new clients who 'get' me and my work.
- After all these years, the postman finally delivers packages to my front door.
- My dog barking after not being able to bark for two years.
- Multiple appearances of my guidance signs.
- Beautiful opportunities.
- Fantastic experiences opening due to cancellations making unexpected experiences available.
- An issue with our accommodation which meant free nights and an extended trip.
- Greater ease channelling mystics.
- Ideas for future writing projects.
- Green lights.
- A surprise trip.
- An ex-student of many decades ago becoming a client.

- It is always a miracle every time I get a clarity-enhancing accurate oracle card reading for clients, I never tire of the magic of it.
- My delayed flight presented as somewhat annoying in the first moment, however, we missed rough weather, and our flight time was reduced by 40 minutes as a quicker route was taken to make up for lost time.
- We experienced a snow event weekend in much sought-after accommodation because many people cancelled as the roads were going to be closed. We didn't get that memo, and it was clear driving up. The blizzard didn't descend until after we arrived.
- Booking a trip and, unbeknownst to us, an old friend was also staying—a surprise for him as well.
- Progress at last on long-term renovations.
- Uplevelled connection with nature.
- My son experiencing winning golfing miracles.
- The rain stopping just when I started my walk.
- A car park available outside the shop I needed to enter.
- Prophetic dreams and messages.
- Many experiences of living the messages contained within this book.
- Improving health and well-being.
- Increasing incidents of wonder and awe.
- My dog living for over 17 amazing years.
- People discovering my books and then reaching out to book online and in person sessions.

MY IGNITION TIP

Upon hearing of another's miracle(s), feel what that would feel like in your heart and mind. Experience miracles vicariously to remind you of their potential and as a prompt for receiving your own 'parallel' miracle. Be in the zone for receiving and tracking your miracles by clearing all that is in the way of your love and peace. This will build the most enduring platform for miracles. Be a graduate of my first two books to help pave the way to the infinite power of your peace, wisdom, love and potential.

ILLUMINATIVE JOURNALLING INQUIRY

What miracles would I most like to receive this month? Before recording your tracked miracles, write out as many miracles as you can imagine as if they have already been delivered. You may like to begin each miracle statement with a 'Thanks for ...' (Insert what you would like to occur here). Expectation, excitement and gratitude in advance are very powerful miracle magnets. For me, this has been a great power behind the manifestation of my miracles. The miracles are already on their way! Truly Miraculous! I will say it again, 'Faith is everything.'

Vibration is Everything

*I am working daily to maintain
my highest possible vibration
through every thought,
word and action.*

We attract what we are; operating at the same frequency of the miracles that we desire is key to magnetising them towards us. We draw in that which vibrates at the same frequency as us. Accepting this as truth is deep motivation to raise one's vibe to truly thrive. The opposite is not as fun or miracle-inducing.

To elevate our vibration, we need to elevate our thoughts, emotions and mood. This becomes our main work and focus until it becomes our new normal. Low vibes void miracles. To raise our vibration, we need to change our tune and change our frequency to the highest degree. Whatever is showing up in our lives is a representation of our vibration. The universe duplicates what we ourselves are radiating in some form or another.

Some quick reminders and practices to absorb for high vibration inducement:

- We raise our vibration every time we choose love. Love connects us with the highest frequency of creation.
- We raise our vibration every time we choose self-care. Our self-care calms us, nurtures us and encourages our growth. Through our self-care, we can gently let go of old limitations, beliefs and stories, thereby opening up to our light in the

process. Our self-care teaches us to respond to life in such a way that elevates our vibration.

- Taking care of our energy system through reiki and other modalities of energy healing clears lower vibrational energies and connects us with the highest possible frequencies. People who make energy healing a part of their life flow through life with greater ease, contentment and with greater occurrence of miracles.

- Nature takes us with her to higher vibrations as she doesn't know how to operate with low vibes. She's happy to help you shift yours when you're in her presence. Let the sun's rays replenish and uplift you.

- Crystals and sage sticks are great for clearing lower vibrations from us and our surroundings.

- Water is the great cleanser of our accumulated energies. Soak in her, swim in her, walk by her, sail on her.

- Avoid judgement and all derivatives of meanness and gossip. Obviously, these modes are the entry to low-vibrational living. Yes, every single time. Don't go there.

- Alcohol is a low vibrational activity as soon as it moves us from the occasional celebratory few drinks into the abyss. Be aware of spending time with people who drink excessively as their low vibes and associated energies infiltrate your energy field. Sometimes after being around toxic people, you can experience an emotional hangover. Be aware that if you are energy-sensitive you can also pick up the energies of places and people that friends have been around. Be mindful of whom and where you spend your time. Clear your energies quickly after these encounters to get back to your own frequency.

- Create and imagine. Creative energy is high vibrational energy.
- Be in service, gifting what you love to the world. You get to not only raise your vibration but that of many others.
- Follow your joy and feel good. This will raise your vibration for attracting your miracles.
- Gratitude is the ultimate vibration raiser. Fall in love with your life and way of living to draw in more. Be grateful for everything! It's all showing up just for you.

MY IGNITION TIP

Honour your vibration. Read *Pearls of Wisdom: For Your Path to Peace* to clear away everything in the way of your peace (high vibration) wisdom, power and potential for creating miracles. Read *Seeds of Self-Care: For Love and Serenity* to activate your love and maintain your highest frequency daily.

ILLUMINATIVE JOURNALLING INQUIRY

Where are the low-vibe experiences in my life and what do I need to do to maintain high vibes?

Wholeness and Miracles

I am whole, and I am complete.

Wholeness is the freedom to be all that we are and all that we can be, with heart, mind, body and soul working coherently as one. Return to your wholeness. It is already within you, awaiting you. To find your wholeness, you must heal yourself.

Wholeness means we have increasing freedom from our shadow aspects and limitations. We also rise above the overwhelming nature of our fear. In wholeness, we learn to accept fear as a background sensation that sometimes arises when we have reached our outer limits of what we have been used to handling and is therefore something to be valued rather than the cause of great despair. There is always room to grow and stretch more when we feel whole. Fear does not become a giant roadblock, just an indication that we are moving beyond our previous comfort threshold in some new way. Celebrate your growing wholeness as you befriend your fear. Allow fear to assist you to access even more wisdom, leading you to even more wholeness.

Making the choice for love moves us along the spiritual path that leads us back to wholeness. Connecting with source energy and accessing our divine connection to love (our true nature) gives us a sense of wholeness. Our wholeness is co-created; we do not achieve this alone. We are never alone, always supported. Allowing love to be the leading force in our lives moves us closer to wholeness.

Wholeness indicates that we know our worth and are willing to receive the bounty that life has to offer. Wholeness means that we have a growing understanding of the ego and its machinations, and we buy into it only momentarily. Our wholeness is stronger than our ego. Through wholeness, we move from karma to dharma, accessing flow, creativity and a prevalence of miracles. In wholeness, we access a state of awareness that embraces and accesses multiple dimensions and the mystical and sacred in all things. We become truly miraculous beings.

Wholeness allows us to feel oneness rather than separation. We feel aligned with our higher selves and higher purpose, connecting with our inner wisdom and intuition. More often (than not) we feel peace, regardless of life's storms.

We empty ourselves of all that is the way of our wholeness. When we are whole and peaceful the world will catch up and follow suit; miracles of all kinds will manifest for humanity.

MY IGNITION TIP

We need to feel whole and worthy of receiving to be in the most attractive and magnetic space for miracles.

ILLUMINATIVE
JOURNALLING INQUIRY

What have I placed in the way of fully stepping
into my state of wholeness?

Worthiness

*I am a miracle, and I am
worthy of miracles.*

Our worth determines our access to miracles. Our worth is a fragile, innocent and precious child until it grows into its adult strength. Surround yourself with those who would champion your self-worth until it blooms into self-love—a deep self-love that cannot be tainted by blame, shame or any derivatives of fear. Through our self-worth and self-love, we will know the miraculous state of freedom and its concurrent power to manifest all manner of miracles.

It has taken me decades to reach the point of recognising that what I allow into my world is a direct representative of my worth. My worth provides the foundation for what I will embrace in life in terms of opportunities and growth experiences. The underlying belief is always centred around, 'Am I worthy of this?' Sabotage creeps in subconsciously if the things we desire feel too big for us. We protect our worth at all costs, often through avoidance and refusal rather than via the self-care and self-love we require for opening to miracles.

My low self-worth manifested as me wishing to remain hidden from the larger world. I would both subconsciously and unconsciously resist all opportunities that would lead to more visibility. From this stance I was avoiding both success and stepping into the full magnitude of me. All moments in our journey through life can lead us back to our worth, love and miracles if that is our intent and desire. This possibility exists for us all regardless of our traumatic backgrounds and conditioned responses. We are that powerful, that miraculous. Worth is built by one thought, one choice, one stretching action at a time. Over time, my self-care showed me how worthy I truly was of love and miracles and changed my brain functioning and nervous system enough to receive miracles. Our self-worth is something to be greatly nurtured as it directly impacts our unconscious decisions around what we can and cannot receive. Self-worth governs what we tell ourselves we deserve.

Our self-worth is our life force. Self-worth either moves us forward toward our inspiration and desires or away from all that we have deemed to be too great and beyond us. The value we place on ourselves is vitally important as it affects our choices, our actions, our decisions, our belief in our dreams, and the trust we have in our ability to create and receive miracles.

All of your choices are an extension of
your perceived self-worth.

Healthy self-worth allows us to trust in the process of our life, knowing it unfolds for our highest good. This stance makes us feel good and feeling good is a magnet for miracles. We know we are supported and surrounded in love and light. As we grow in worth, we find that the ego quietens, and we step into our greater purpose and best service. A subdued ego loses its ability to convince us to stay small, fit in and accept anything less than our best life—and that is miraculous. We trust our role in the grand scheme of things, connecting more to oneness rather than separation. Our self-worth allows us to experience freedom from comparison and envy, taking us to the place of being able to celebrate the success of others: a double miracle. The worthier we feel, the greater the light we allow in and the more we radiate our energy-changing presence to others. Our worth ignites our inner light to the point of being able to generate miracles: blessings of all kinds. Self-worth is a superpower.

Worthiness is a magnet for miracles, healing and abundance of all kinds. Affirm your worth every moment of every day. It is an essential ingredient of miracles.

Know deeply within:
I am worthy of my power, light, peace and love.
I am worthy of money.
I am worthy of success.
I am worthy of abundance.
I am worthy of great love.
I am worthy of miracles of all kinds.
I am worthy of synchronistic beautiful events, drawing to me all that I desire and require.
I am worthy of joy.
I am worthy of doors opening to new opportunities.
I am worthy of adventure.
I am worthy of beautiful relationships.
I am worthy of excitement.
I am worthy of optimal health.
I am worthy of an expansive, meaningful, purposeful life.
I am worthy of life-changing inspiration and creativity.
I am worthy of peace.

I am worthy of my innate, powerful wisdom.
I am worthy of nurturing, healing, uplifting self-care.
I am worthy of my connection with nature.
I am worthy of being seen and heard and respected.
I am worthy of all my talents and abilities, those known and yet to be discovered.
I am worthy of beauty, receiving and gifts of all kinds.

MY IGNITION TIP

Befriend your self-worth. Nurture and encourage it as you would a small child. Talk with your inner child, reminding them of all that is wonderful and amazing about them.

ILLUMINATIVE JOURNALLING INQUIRY

What am I so worthy of that I am currently resisting?
If my self-worth was extraordinary, what would I choose for myself?

Write a Letter to
the Universe

*I am in direct contact with
universal love and guidance. I
listen, and I am heard.*

The universe is phenomenal, as are you. It loves you and would like to explicitly know what you require and desire most in life. It struggles to keep up with what it picks up via your ever-changing thoughts, feelings and emotions. The messages often get scrambled.

A great way to communicate clearly with the magical ethers is to write a letter to the universe. In this way, you are fine-tuning your request frequency. I include an experience of letter writing in *Pearls of Wisdom: For Your Path to Peace*. I had not been in a relationship for many years and had made the demand on myself that a new relationship was going to be great, or I was not having one at all. I had a dozen or more 'criteria' around the personal qualities I would most desire to have in my new man. The last criteria was that I wanted a whole man, someone who was sorted within himself. Suffice to say, my future husband's surname was Holman and he's the most 'whole' man I've encountered. The miraculous nature of this was that the universe 'delivered' my man with far more amazing qualities than I could ever have 'designed'.

The universe is unlimited, and we need to embrace this knowledge to create miracles. Please try this letter writing to the universe out for yourself, and not just about relationships. Sit quietly with yourself and decide what is most pressing right now. The universe is open for small requests as well as large ones. Writing out your letter and then carrying out some kind of ritual around it (perhaps burning it or leaving it in moonlight, under the stars) makes your request sacred and magical and is delivered to the heart of the universe. Sometimes it is the simplest, purest, most heartfelt acts that draw in our miracles with greater rapidity.

You may also wish to try writing a thank you letter in advance to the universe stating your gratitude for the arrival of your currently desired miracle. There is great power in believing a desire is already on its way for us. Writing letters to the universe and having them answered for our highest good (for they will be) builds our trust in our personal creative power and in the wonder and inherent benevolence of the universe.

Another way to draw in miracles is having two or more individuals behind the same dream—such is the power of combined intention, great love and consciousness: prayer-like. I'm going to support my husband's current dream by writing a letter to the universe on his behalf.

Dear universe,

My husband is the best man I know. He continually gives to others and at the same time knows how to dream big and manifest. My life with him is always one of fun, adventure and great possibility—which I am extremely grateful for every day. He provides livelihoods for many men and women and shows great generosity of spirit to his family, always freely giving his time and resources. You can see where I'm going with this, dear universe, I'm asking for a miracle of magnitude to match him! Over the last couple of years, his love of sailing and the associated freedom and ability to explore unknown beautiful locations has resurfaced and expanded. He has a beautiful catamaran on the very top of his bucket list. Please can this boat be his, occurring in the best timeframe with the most beautiful unfolding process and journey. I wish to see him thrilled with his new boat.

Thank you in advance! I can't wait to share in his happiness and start our adventuring on the seas.

I am love and gratitude beyond measure,

Jane xxx

MY IGNITION TIP

Believe in the power and benevolence of the universe. Belief is everything and a necessary and powerful force behind our miracles. Believe wholeheartedly in having the universal requests (in your letter) delivered.

ILLUMINATIVE JOURNALLING INQUIRY

What are my most secret desires and miracle requests?

You Are Not Your Mind

I am the sovereign and the power behind my miracle-inducing mind.

You are not your mind; you are the observer of it and the creator of it. Program it well, for if not, it will program you—most likely from an ego standpoint and perhaps not for your highest good. Witness everything with your being, not your mind. You don't need its commentary, it is limited, you are not.

Step back from thyself to free thyself. Avoid being drawn into the ramblings of the mind. It has been a little unwell for some time as you forgot to take the reins and manage it, so it became a little out of control and uneasy. It may have bolted temporarily but you can take charge and reclaim yourself. Avoid allowing your mind to take over your life. You deserve more than the ruination an untrained mind can bring to you and your life. Take back your awareness, observe the mind in action; don't become the mind. You are the orchestrator of how your mind functions.

Our minds will complain about and negatively judge everything and anything if we allow it. It needs great instructions to help you be in the right space to create miracles. It awaits your command and ownership, otherwise, it never reaches its potential as a great ally and creator of your reality. If you don't teach it positive habits, it will always keep you small and in a state of unease, anxiety, doubt or fear. The ego attempts to keep you fearful in an inadvertent attempt to keep you safe, so you won't have to be too amazing and step into something 'scary' like your true greatness. The ego is afraid (for you) of your greatness. Eventually, with enough encouragement in the form of re-direction, it will quieten and allow you to be all of you: the expansive version of you.

Start the mind training process with your thoughts today. Each thought has the potential to impact your emotional state. An elevated feel-good state is most conducive to your miracles. Allow your heart and mind to do their best work with congruence and awareness as the predominant co-factors, working powerfully as one.

Get to know your ego and its strategies well. Sometimes its modus operandi is overt and at other times it's entirely covert; this is when your conscious awareness is most needed to continue steering you and your life in the direction of miracles. You will come to know when your ego is at play. Your self-worth may swing to self-importance or it may conversely move to doubt, fear, comparison or even jealousy. As you tune in over time, there will be signals in your body and psyche such as feelings of unease or fear that will let you know the ego is no longer firmly in the backseat where it should be. The ego will not ignite your light and unleash your miracles, only you are powerful enough for that. You will know you are back in alignment with your highest self when you are in a place of gratitude for all that you are and all that you receive, and you can surrender and flow without being vested in outcomes.

Claiming authority over our minds and programming it expertly is essential for scripting our miracles. Being the observer of our minds, stepping back and being the awareness—the one who is watching the thoughts—is life-changing and miracle-inducing. In this space, we are using our minds to create our lives rather than limiting them or allowing them to evolve randomly and uselessly at whim. Choosing the content of our thoughts and directing when, where and in what format they are allowed to flow, is consciousness in evidence. Fostering sovereignty of our minds allows us to discern if messages are coming from our higher self, versus originating within the egoic mind. We get to be the observer of our reactions: seeing the gifts, potential learning, and gateway to freedom within the tests we experience.

We use our minds with greater purpose when we avoid giving our attention to unnecessary things that make us feel bad. Redirect and reroute your thoughts towards greater proactivity and positivity. Avoid allowing your precious energy to be wasted or harmful to you. Use your attention to heal you and move you towards greater health and happiness.

MY IGNITION TIP

Love your mind back to wellness. Observe its antics and support its potential as you would a young, innocent child. Create your life rather than worry about your life. Use your thoughts and associated energy powerfully and wisely to ignite your light and create your miracles. Forgive your mind its indiscretions and encourage it to move in a new direction with you as the captain steering the ship. Celebrate your awakening.

ILLUMINATIVE JOURNALLING INQUIRY

How can I observe with my being this day,
rather than allowing the mind to run its
usual commentary?
Where has my thinking been taking me that
I no longer desire to go?
Where am I now taking my thinking to
support the creation of my miracles?

You Are the Miracle You've Been Waiting For: Claim You

I had a deep sense over a couple of weeks that a life-changing miracle was coming my way. I will admit I went straight to materialistic options: the TattsLotto win; massive international book sales; the prize home; the dream trip—I'm sure you know how it goes.

The miracle was delivered in a very 'unexpected' format.

What proceeded was the most tumultuous weeks of inner turmoil that I could remember. Interestingly enough, this experience coincided with a blood moon eclipse.

I was fuelled by a relentless, unpleasant adrenaline-like state. I was not tired for one moment over a period of about 5 days, even at night-time I was wired and had only spasmodic sleep. I worried about anything and everything I had ever worried about in this lifetime and went into self-doubt and feelings of unworthiness. I pictured myself being in a cocoon and being pushed through some kind of birth canal. I remember the day I emerged out of it, I felt free of the old me and set free to enjoy the authentic me. There was a sense of not caring about anything that wasn't aligned with me and how I wanted to be and feel. I could no longer go to the space of stressing and fretting and doubting and worrying. I was done. I had now discovered the miracle of me. I was peaceful, strong, confident, self-loving and more committed than ever to shining in my life and living my purpose. The interesting thing was that a person very close to me had his own 'epiphany'. This radical turnaround occurred on the same day I 'emerged' and changed a life path that had existed for a decade that was no longer in alignment with the man he had become. Miracles are beautifully contagious; such is our energetic connection to others.

Miracle me has stepped back into greater surrender and now mostly lets life and my intuition lead. The older version of me (whom I also loved as she led me to *me*) finally let go so I could find the miracle of me. When we discover our own miraculous nature, we are at our most powerful for activating and receiving miracles. We are no longer aligned with limiting stories, thinking patterns and beliefs. Miracles occur that inspire us (and others) to become even more of who we are, allowing new talents and abilities to emerge that change us and those around us. We live our beautiful, destined lives, open to all that life wants to gift to us for our highest good. We live through love as infinite beings of unlimited potential. We see and experience miracles as our natural way of being. Desires that are created within, manifest into our reality. Our wishes that may have seemed pure fantasy can, at last, materialise for the enjoyment of all. Set you free to be all of you: a living, breathing inspirational miracle.

MY IGNITION TIP

Claim the miracle of you today. Make this demand
to yourself. Now is the time, there is no reason to
wait. Intent will show you the way.

ILLUMINATIVE
JOURNALLING INQUIRY

Are you willing to go within to find that which
prevents you from emerging from your own
cocoon and meeting the miracle you?
What would you have to see, face and release
today to take your first baby step?

You Only Get One Body

*I am the loving guide, supporter
and healer of my body.*

Our bodies are living, breathing miracles. Take a moment to pause and reflect on everything your body gifts to you in a day and everything it allows you to do and achieve. It is almost beyond comprehension. Reflect on your body's greatness. It appreciates your gratitude, love and respect. It is the greatest vessel you will experience throughout your life—a most miraculous ride.

We can have many things in this lifetime, but we only get one body so it is in our best interests to look after it if we would like it to help us create miracles. Every day we either nurture or hinder our body with the choices we make moment to moment. Each thought either infuses our cells with healing and inspiration or diminishes their functioning. Every morsel of food or drink either nourishes or impairs our immune system and bodily functioning.

Allow your light to transform your physical body. The greater the amount of light our bodies can hold, the lighter we feel and the higher our vibration is for drawing in miracles. The light within us heals our bodies and at the same time radiates out into the world around us. Also consider that light-filled beings require less energy in the form of food, giving our bodies greater time for optimum functioning, rather than food processing.

Practise loving your body so that it can be your most powerful vehicle for driving and delivering you miracles.

Each day love some aspect of your body to elevate its healing capacity and enhance your bodily connection. The greater your connection is with your body, the more you will develop your ability to listen to its whispers. You will begin to understand what the physical symptoms within your body are attempting to communicate with you. Start small if this is initially too confronting. Practise loving your hair, your eyes, and your ability to walk, see, hear or smell. There is always something to love. Practise loving your body to practise loving you. After some time, loving bodily attention will become automatic and conducive to optimal wellbeing.

'How I love thee, let me count the ways.'
\- Elizabeth Barrett Browning

MY IGNITION TIP

Forge a new relationship with your body.
Consider the needs of your body in every thought,
word and action. Love your body and it will
respond with improved wellness and vitality.

ILLUMINATIVE JOURNALLING INQUIRY:

Dear Body,
What do you require for optimal well-being this day? What would you like to ingest? How would you like to move? What would you like to experience?

What can I love about my body today? Challenge yourself with the lengthiest list you can compile.

Your Version of Amazing

I am amazing, and the world now discovers and enjoys how amazing I am.

Everyone has their own version of amazing when their light is ignited. Our amazingness unleashes our light and our miracles. It is our job as miracle workers to discover how amazing we are and to share our most amazing and miraculous selves with others through our contributions to life. Through our willingness to step into our amazingness, our darker shadow aspects and our self-imposed unique set of limitations have been brought to the surface for healing. They are no longer the dominant aspects in play. We transcend fear and step into our potential.

There is enough room for everyone's version of amazingness, and I'm convinced that when you start seeing your own version of amazing you notice it more in others. There are women that have been in my life for years but somehow in recent years, they seem to have become more extraordinary to me in who they are and the way they operate in life. There are some women who have the gift of humour, some who present themselves impeccably and creatively in the world and some who have survived the most extreme health battles and personal challenges. Some are great speakers, captivating others with their eloquence. Some are brilliant connectors and entertainers. Some cook the most delectable dishes. Some teach and heal and counsel in the most transformative of ways. Some are natural mothers with thriving children. The list is endless. Start appreciating your own circle of amazing people. Light igniting is contagious and transformational on so many levels. Imagine a world where each person ignited their own light. Miracles would become the new normal.

MY IGNITION TIP

Make a list of some of your favourite women (known and unknown to you personally) and their amazing qualities. Go through this list and circle any of the qualities you perceive you also have. If you are noticing these qualities then it is highly likely you possess these same attributes, you may just not have acknowledged them until now. Well done, you are one step closer to claiming miraculous you.

ILLUMINATIVE JOURNALLING INQUIRY

What is truly amazing about me?
Don't think about it, just write.
Celebrate your list and, most importantly, all that you are.

PART 2

MESSAGES FROM THE MYSTICS:

GODS, GODDESSES & OTHERWORLDLY BEINGS

There have been wise ones, ancient ones and mystical ones from all times, space and dimensions who have taken Earth into their hands and hearts and gifted us with knowledge. This knowledge frees and moves us to greater love and wholeness, to a state where head, heart, mind, body and spirit work together as one. Magic and miracles are boundless and timeless. Tune into the mystics for a great remembering of what may be possible for you and your life.

I use the term 'mystic' loosely to encompass the many divine beings who wished to express their beautiful truths and insight into miracles through this work. My gratitude and awe know no bounds. For the purpose of this book, I consider mystics as beings who have woven the sacred and spiritual into their lives or connected with their inner sacred upon passing. Regardless, they are committed to enhancing all of humanity from whatever dimension they now occupy.

The mystics that have shown up for us here with all their innate and earned wisdom are helping to draw us closer to our own mystical and miraculous personas. Mystics are powerful in infusing us with great wisdom, providing us with keys to unlock us and a new world—a greater way of being and living. These beings connect us with all that is possible in the unknown mystical world of miracles. They lead us to what is possible, even when we don't know what that is... yet. They live and breathe the sacred and are helping to infuse this essence into our existence. They have transcended the physical to embrace the freedom of enlightened states. They have awoken to the truth of themselves and to the workings of the universe as they know it so far.

My focus has been on the messages from the mystics that came through for me, for you, and not on their life stories. There is so much information available on their respective stories, much of which is open to interpretation and possibly embellished over time according to who has researched and written about them. I also feel many ancient mystics have been misrepresented or misinterpreted due to the limitations of awareness and understanding back in time. All who showed up for this book have love in their hearts and an enlightened way of seeing all that was, all that is, and all that is to come.

I chose to not focus on the past of the mystics showing up to speak with us as they have evolved significantly since earlier times and are no longer defined by their origins or past incarnations. Many of the mystics who came through for us chose their own titles. Like us, many of these mystics are more concerned with who they are becoming rather than who they were centuries or lifetimes ago. The power is in the present and all beings continue to evolve. Each now exists in higher frequency dimensions with ever-evolving, complex roles. Their messages are what is important for us at this moment in time.

These beings are committed to attaining insight into the mysteries for transcending human knowledge:

connecting with the divine, activating cosmic awareness and potential, and sharing this with us. We are invited to witness the sacred within ourselves and all of life and to remember our spiritual origins for creating our most powerful, miraculous living for the betterment of all. Miracles abound. Allow the mystics to lead you towards your miracles.

This section will require your most open heart and mind. Receive what feels light and right for you. Connect with the energy, the essence of each being, and you will have an experience beyond words. Cultivate an awareness of time outside our current understanding. In channelling these messages, there was no timeframe given, simply a reflection on possibilities as we evolve as a species of divine, cosmic beings. I feel we have been given sage insight into what we require for our next steps, and also a glimpse into what may be possible on the horizons of consciousness for humankind.

We are all mystics in the making, capable of perceiving the sacredness woven into the fabric of our very existence throughout the past, present and future. Mystics connect with the earth and the stars, forging new awareness through the power of both realms. They know we are one with it all. They see through conscious eyes, always acknowledging that all is not as it seems and often so much more than we can perceive. Mystics contemplate all and self-reflect to surrender to it all. They understand that we are powerful spiritual beings having an equally powerful earthly existence. They surrender to that which is beyond the intellect to the magical, mystical synchronicity of life.

There are often no words to describe mystical experiences as they are perceived with all the senses—and those that are only just developing within humankind—and have an ineffable quality. They arise almost spontaneously with no effort; they just are. Mystical experiences give us an intuitive understanding of the meaning of existence. There is such peace, power and clarity involved in the mystical. Embracing the sacred is a birthplace for miracles. We infinitely expand our consciousness opening portals to our mystical world.

What common threads can you perceive woven through these mystical messages for advancing our love, awareness, potential and tendency towards miracle?

Embrace the mysterious to embrace the miraculous.

Aine
Irish Goddess

The place of miracles often requires moving into a new space to receive them. You may be required to enter many unknown domains, creating yourself anew. If your miracle desires are large and life-changing, who do you need to become to meet them?

What you are choosing and simultaneously radiating outwards is directly proportional to the miracles that you will draw in. Accept this truth and you will place more energy behind the uplevelling of you, and for your efforts, you may even reach for dreams that you had previously decided were beyond you.

Nothing is limited if you believe in yourself and make choices that align with who you are becoming, rather than who you once were.

Be adaptable in life: change anything in a heartbeat, including yourself. Re-invent and re-create as often as you choose. You have permission. Avoid allowing you or your life to become set in stone. There is just too much to be experienced for the unfolding miracle-makers reading this book. Stay awake to possibility. Miracles are around the next corner, make that turn, take the long winding path.

MY IGNITION TIP

Set great new intentions for yourself around how
you will show up and create this new life. Grant
yourself the gift of deeply believing your life can be
different: richer, more luscious, more adventurous
and ever-changing.

ILLUMINATIVE
JOURNALLING INQUIRY

Who do I need to become to meet my miracles?
What actions will I take?
What beliefs about me will I change?
What beliefs about my life will I need to change?

Andromedins
Star Beings

Love and cherish all of your life to draw in your best life. Make your life an adventure. Feel free to be free. Look up, look around and see with fresh eyes all that is truly wondrous in existence around you. It does not matter if life is not what you would consider to be so wonderful for you now. All you need to do is see and acknowledge any form of wonder, even if it is happening on the other side of the world for other individuals. This will begin your connection to a greater way of being and living.

All that is not 'wonderful' is most often an illusion of your own making. Lift your own veil of obscurity to set yourself free to be all that you intend for this lifetime. As you are all connected, tap into the frequency of those you admire to teach yourself what it may feel and be like to live a life filled with wonder and awe. Find awe in a waterfall, in the design of a ladybird, in the texture of snow or in the magical power of a flame. You must teach yourself how to be and how to make your life an adventure worth living. All of your busyness and stress is how you keep your destined life away from you. Be willing to stop and discover your greatness and the true life that is calling you. You will find it underneath all of your unresolved issues and the stuff you accumulate around you in place of connecting with yourself, your love and an awe-filled way of living. You need to be willing to be all that you desire. There is no more time to waste. There is an urgency now on Earth. There is a mass calling for change and even radical transformation. Your miracles are demanding that you show up for them.

Now is the time, and it is most certainly your time. Will you heed the call?

My answer: a resounding yes. Please join me and let a new wave of life start to flow and glow throughout our world.

MY IGNITION TIP

Seek moments of wonder this day and every day thereafter. Start with what is around you and then broaden your view. Perhaps start a tracking wonder journal. Track your moments of wonder to encourage being able to move into states of awe, those stop-you-in-your-tracks, totally present moments. Being in a state of awe is a miracle that few seek but is available to many.

ILLUMINATIVE JOURNALLING INQUIRY

What can I now see that will connect me with wonder?

Aphrodite
Greek Goddess

Fall in love with yourself and all of life. Let love be the power and magic behind your miracles. Embrace the miracle of discovering your bliss and beauty. Beauty is a miracle for those willing to see and feel it. Beauty softens life and connects us with love. Find beauty wherever you can, in whatever you can. It might be in the flow of a skirt, in the sparkling eyes of a loved one when they greet you, it might be witnessed through rain cleansing the earth, it might be experienced through beautiful words or a beautiful creation.

Beauty is within us all and for us all. Nature will always gift us beauty, revel in its gifts. Connect with the beauty in nature to open to its power within yourself.

Your task is to find your unique avenues for experiencing, witnessing and creating beauty. Beauty can be your first foray into the world of miracles. Love your beauty and your beauty will love you, unlocking the miracle of self-worth. Beauty will change you within, allowing your miracle manifestation power to be ignited.

MY IGNITION TIP

Make seeking and connecting with beauty of all kinds a focus of your days: beauty in yourself, others, nature and all things.

ILLUMINATIVE JOURNALLING INQUIRY

What new elements of my beauty can
I open to now?

Apollo
Greek God

You are stronger than you give yourself credit for and you have all that you require within to navigate your way through life towards your miracles. Physical and emotional strength of the highest degree is required during these days on Earth.

Your physical fortitude , is enhanced by optimal emotional wellbeing. Feeling good predisposes you to make choices that enhance your health and accompanying lifestyle. Manage your mind to manage your health on all levels.

Take great care of your physical body as it is the only vessel you have for transporting your powerful soul. A strong body encourages a strong mind, the two have a symbiotic relationship. Move your body. Allow it to recalibrate in the sun and in nature.

Your life and the world around benefit greatly from the power of you: physically, emotionally, spiritually and mentally. Taking the ultimate care of these four elements allows for your light to be fully ignited and your miracles unleashed.

The way to develop your strength using one emotional muscle at a time is to focus on your strengths, not on any perceived weaknesses. The energy that you have available each day needs to be used to serve you well, and focusing on what is not working can not only detract from your life and wellbeing but also draw to you more of what you do not desire. That is how powerful you are, my friend. Fuel your miracles with thoughts of your greatness and align your actions accordingly.

MY IGNITION TIP

Treat your body as a temple.
Regularly clear your mind of unwelcome weeds.
Nurture your emotional body back to your
greatest health.
Know yourself; connect with guidance and
honour your wonderful attributes for these
connect you with your miracles.

ILLUMINATIVE
JOURNALLING INQUIRY

What evidence of my strengths
do I have in life?

Arcturians
Star Beings

The light is the way, the only way.

The path of light has been complex, challenging and hazardous for what seems like eons. Honour the brave souls throughout time who have done the work to be harbingers of change. These pioneers, courageous explorers and seeds of the new are relishing in being witness to the changes occurring not only for Earth but for the cosmos, for we are all one. Creative chaos is evidence of many people's desires for more in this world. The miracles are increasing:

- Man is sensing the interconnectedness of all things and making choices that serve the whole.
- Mother Earth is being recognised and honoured, healing many things.
- The frequency of love is reverberating around the globe with increasing strength.
- Healing within, which then heals the outer world, is occurring with unprecedented strength.
- Humankind is opening up to previously obscure talents and abilities.
- Ego domination is giving way to higher self-empowerment and awareness.
- The veil between worlds is thinning, allowing for much consciousness to be filtered onto the planet.
- Higher dimensional beings will 'walk' the earth, increasing its vibration in unprecedented ways.

My Ignition Tip

Out of chaos comes great opportunities for creativity and change. Look beneath the surface of chaotic events to see a deeper truth. Perhaps chaos is a prelude to miracles.

Illuminative Journalling Inquiry

What chaos within my life and in the world can I now perceive as things 'volcanically erupting' to be released?

Arianrhod
Celtic Goddess

Trust in the timing of all things in your life. There is always time; it will expand for you if you connect with it rather than attempt to control it. Be at one with, and at peace with time.

Patience is a miracle creating flow and therefore potent possibility. Going against the tides of life moves you against creation and against miracles. Ebb and flow with the tides. Wax and wane with the moon. Bloom and fall with the leaves.

The unfolding of miracles, the process and the journey are as important as desired outcomes. Many miracles occur along the way to miracles. Be grateful for all that occurs to stir the potential for more.

Each day provides the possibility of a rebirth of sorts. What once was does not have to be true for you now. Recreate yourself anew as often as you choose. Become free of time and the past. Release any stories that tie you to a past that you do not wish to replicate. Be in today for it is where your miracles arise.

Connect with the energy of miracles by harnessing the power of nature. Draw inwards the potency of crashing waves, a cascading waterfall, a volcanic eruption, or gale force winds. You are nature in all her elements. Some days you may be a light breeze and on other occasions you may be a gathering tsunami. Gather all of your forces for your miracles. Your life needs all of you and all your seasons.

MY IGNITION TIP

Ask to move into the space where time expands
and see what you can create.

ILLUMINATIVE
JOURNALLING INQUIRY

Where can patience contribute to my
miracles on this day?

Athena
Greek Goddess

Self-knowledge is your greatest power right now. Know yourself to liberate yourself. All miracles arise from the light and awareness within you. All that you have experienced has led you to all that you have become. You are in the best position of your life to open to more: more knowledge, more healing, more power and more potential. There is no endpoint to what you can evolve into and create once you are unlocked. Face the uncertainty, face the unease, for it is your wisdom revealing itself to you and for you. Step into the unknown version of yourself with great anticipation and confidence.

What is your strategy for waging war on darkness and igniting your light?

Will you finally speak your truth?

Suppressing yourself does not invoke miracle you.

Will you choose work that lights you up?

Choosing work that is not great for you diminishes the possibility of a powerful 'miracle you' revealing herself.

Will you, at last, forgive to be free?

Lack of forgiveness is just another way you keep small, it's an excuse for staying stuck and keeping your disempowering victim story in play.

Will you say no to all that is not aligning with your beliefs and inherent values?

People-pleasing is another way of avoiding the awareness and power of you.

Will you feel your global nature rather than your 'my place, my space' nature?

Staying inside a contained box where not many beings get to experience you does not release miracle you.

Will you conquer your long-held, self-imposed and self-governing fears?

You allow your fears to exist to provide you with brick walls to prevent your miracles from arising within you and for you.

Break free of the prison walls you have built for yourself. There is no one else to blame for anything that is evident in your life because you have drawn it all towards yourself to reveal you, to you. Clever you! Own it, acknowledge it. What a powerful creator you are. Now you've got all 'that' out of the way, what would you really like to create? What is your new life looking and feeling like? What miracles do you plan on manifesting starting today? The present is the time.

This lifetime's work is on you. You, powerful you, in all your deep shades and glory, is what you have been waiting for this whole time.

Are you ready to meet you? All of you?

The canvas of your life will radically alter when you are ready to step into being you. Miracles begin or end with you. Claim your divine birthright to unleash your miracles.

MY IGNITION TIP

Athena packs a conscious miracle-inducing punch.
She inspires me to let go of all the self-imposed
'nonsense'... what about you?
Are you ready to meet powerful miracle you on
the other side of all the illusionary, strength-
obscuring falsity and the unreal and untrue
versions of you?

ILLUMINATIVE
JOURNALLING INQUIRY

The commitment: I am meeting the authentic,
miracle-manifesting me today.
What powerful attributes and abilities can I claim
today that I have previously concealed from myself?

Artemis
Greek Goddess

Focus your attention on what is calling to you now. This energy is connecting you with your arising miracles. There is great potential surrounding you now. New opportunities, new directions and new experiences are circling your world, waiting for you to call them out of orbit and into your reality. Be ready to meet this newness and claim it as your own: light ignited, miracles unleashed.

Trust your guidance as it is extremely powerful at this time. Sideline distraction. Stay alert for signs, coincidence and synchronicity: your miracles are making their potential known to you. Soften and surrender to what is releasing within you and leaving your life and at the same time surrender to what is coming—all that you have been calling forth with your new energy. Clear away background noise and connect deeply with what right now brings meaning and a sense of purpose to your world. Let inspiration and heightened feelings guide you along destiny's path. Channel your energy with precision for maximum effectiveness.

Seek inner clarity:

What desires to be birthed through you?

What is the focus of your aim?

What do you have in your sight?

Where is your energy most needed?

What is your next step?

What will your miracle-filled life be like?

How do you choose to feel as you step into your miracle persona?

Shoot for the stars, for they await your light to join with theirs. Shine for this world and for your personal world. Miracles are beautifully bright.

MY IGNITION TIP

Your intention and attention can be superpowers.
Use each most effectively.

ILLUMINATIVE JOURNALLING INQUIRY

What new opportunity would I like to open just for me? What baby step can I take today towards bringing it to fruition?

Benzai-Ten
Japanese Goddess

Beauty is everywhere just waiting for you to see it. Beauty is a miracle because it is an expression of love. When witnessing beauty, we are connecting with the loving, most elevated essence of whatever is before us. We are training ourselves to see the miraculous not only in what may be considered extraordinary but also, and most importantly, in the ordinary. We can learn to find magic and wonder within us and around us in all situations and experiences. We lower our threshold for feeling and being amazing, thus inviting in the miraculous with corresponding ease.

Being the truth of you, the most authentic you, is the greatest expression of your beauty as it represents who you are at your most loving centre. Allow the true miracles within you to be seen by others. Miracles are for sharing.

MY IGNITION TIP

One of the best forms of self-care is learning to perceive and receive beauty wherever we can. Connecting with beauty encourages us to also see it within. The most cared-for and nourished version of you will always be the most miraculous. See your beauty and you are seeing your light.

ILLUMINATIVE
JOURNALLING INQUIRY

Where is the beauty within me?
Where is the beauty in my home surroundings?
Where is the beauty in my outdoor environment?
Where is the beauty in my relationships?

Branwen
Celtic Goddess
of Love

Dear friends,

I wish to acknowledge your amazing efforts to ignite your light and radiate it out into the world.

Love is the miracle.

How will you share your love with the world?

Will you connect with your own beauty and be beautiful in mind and action?

Will you change the world of another by showering this blessed individual with your love?

Will you bring beautiful creations into the world as an expression of your love?

Will you choose something for yourself today just because it brings you joy?

Will you weave the sacred and the mystical into your life to merge more fully with your potential for miracles?

Will you forgive those who don't deserve or care about your forgiveness so your precious energy can be free of them?

Will you become excited about your new life and activate your gifts?

Will you believe in yourself and in the unlimited nature of your potential?

Will you become a living miracle?

MY IGNITION TIP

Where is your love?
Celebrate all there is to love about you, and in
doing so, you will open up to the other parts of
yourself that also need loving.

ILLUMINATIVE
JOURNALLING INQUIRY

Where will I allow love to lead me on this day?

Brigid
Irish Goddess

Owning and sharing one's gifts is the true miracle. Each person is a container for miracles. Be a clear, open conduit for miracles by freeing yourself of all illusions and falsehoods that tell you that you are anything but powerful and worthy.

Miracles shared draw even more miracles into the life of the bestower. Release yourself and your gifts into the world. Burn away all that is in the way of receiving and being the power that is your birthright. Your power and your light ignite your miracles.

What kinds of miracles are you here to create and release this lifetime?

Are you the miracle of free, truthful, and authentic speech and expression?

Are you the miracle of compassion?

Are you the miracle of unconditional love?

Are you the miracle behind the alchemy of the written word?

Are you the miracle of inviting and invoking change?

Are you the miracle of being nature's advocate?

Are you the miracle of changing the energy in a room?

Are you the miracle of presence?

Are you the miracle of going where no person has gone before?

Are you the miracle of hope and optimism?

Are you the miracle of uplifting entertainment?

Are you fire on Earth burning away what is no longer needed?

Are you the miracle of portals, bringing in new energies?

Are you the miracle of seeking the truth and forging new paths for those who cannot?

Are you the miracle of seeing what is written in the stars?

Are you the miracle of unlocking ancient wisdom and soul gifts?

Or... are you the miracle of bringing heaven one step closer to Earth?

Find your inner spark, ignite it and claim your miracle persona today,
Love Brigid x

MY IGNITION TIP

Nourish your self-worth through whatever means are necessary to know you are worthy of your miracles. Surround yourself with those who encourage your worth and light.

ILLUMINATIVE JOURNALLING INQUIRY

Who and what is most conducive to my self-worth right now?

Buddha
Mystic &
Ascended Master

Be still and contemplative to receive yourself and become open to miracles. A miracle appearing in the outer world always has its origins within you. The prevalence of miracles is reflective of the state of one's inner world.

Allow the power and love that is within you to come to the light. Find your golden core underneath all the rubble: the noise, the busyness, the distractions, the outer experiences. Return to your essence, the cosmic heart of you. Attune to the heartbeat of the universe, for it will show you the way. Enlightenment is closer than you think and is co-created: as above, so below.

Hold lightly to this world, knowing that all things, other than your heart centre, are not permanent.

Know what is unreal in life to meet what is real. All that is fear is unreal. Release fear to release suffering. Move through your suffering to release your karma and move into your dharma: your true destined life aligned with cosmic love.

MY IGNITION TIP:

Be your own enlightened teacher. All knowledge
for you and your passage through life is within. Be
quiet and still enough to hear the whispers
of your soul.
Allow your fear to be a guide, showing you what
can be released to move forward. Fear does not
need to be a limitation. Fear can be a sign that you
are challenging your old paradigms and bravely
charting some new territory.

ILLUMINATIVE JOURNALLING INQUIRY:

What does my heart wish to share
with me this day?

Cerridwyn
Celtic Goddess

Your potential is unlimited.

You can read this powerful statement, but you need to feel into it and be open to it so it can bypass the part of your mind that won't allow it to be true. You are worthy of all that you can envision; work your mind to unlock your magic and miracles.

You can be anything you imagine to achieve your highest good and unfolding purpose and destiny. Convince your mind of this truth and you will have freedom. Managing your mind allows you to feel into your heart to ignite your love and spread your light. Your mind is the gatekeeper. Find your key and allow the golden gates to open to your possibility and potential.

MY IGNITION TIP

Avoid allowing your capacity to be muted by living through the crazy mind maze. Live from your heart. A heart-led life is a miracle-filled life.

ILLUMINATIVE
JOURNALLING INQUIRY:

What is my mind telling me that is no
longer true for me?
Write out what is now true for you.

Council
of Light

Team of
Ascended Masters

✦

Less is more.

As you evolve, you will come to gratefully and peacefully see that less is infinitely more. Inner peace is possible from the space of less: less worrying, less doing, less controlling, less forcing and less fear of making decisions. You will learn to focus on what is most important: your inner climate and concurrent responses to life, and the connection with your most powerful higher self. The things you accumulate (whilst enjoyable) are not a reflection of what is most important: your functioning as a being. Your possessions often serve as a great distraction (or addiction) keeping you from realising all of 'you'.

Looking outside of yourself for joy does not make joy a permanent state, it will always be fleeting and depend on the next accumulated 'whatever' to feel contentment again. Make your potential the 'more' and your possessions, 'the less'. Avoid allowing your possessions to possess you. Less (being more) allows productivity to expand as more space is created to just be. Just being allows the more of you to reveal itself to serve you and the world. You can hear and perceive the truth of yourself. Stressing, acquiring and rushing achieves the very opposite of what is desired and simultaneously pushes miraculous occurrences and moments of pure ease and total flow further away.

Connect with your essence, go within to find you and free you. From here, your concern for what goes on around you will be radically reduced as your inner peace will be paramount: pure gold in fact. You will feel so good that you will draw effortlessly to you what your (true) heart desires and that which is for your highest good. Your natural state will have the chance to shine and create. You will feel less like a masquerading imposter and more authentically and truthfully you. There will be less unease, less low vibrational functioning, more peace, more wonder and more miracles. Connect with love moment to moment to find your equivalent of less being more. Time will expand just for you as you do seemingly less, thus creating more time for you and what you love. Allow your miracles to unfold as you intrinsically connect with the universal truth that less is magically more. Outer world miracles are birthed in the inner world.

Be the energetic match of that which you desire to call in.

Be the energy of what you want to receive. Everything in this world has a vibration. To bring something into your reality you must exist on the same frequency. You merge with the energy of the object or experience you desire to bring into your existence. You understand the power of peace and love in creating the experience of your life. Now it is time to use these forces to be and create miracles. You're going to reach higher than you've ever reached before. Now the fun begins.

So, as an example, you have your heart set on a beautiful waterside home. Take yourself there. Immerse yourself in the very fibre of the home. What does it look like? How does it feel to be inside this home? What wonder, awe and gratitude do you have for everything you are seeing and feeling? Take a virtual tour. What can you touch and smell? What senses are activated? You now believe that this spectacular home is yours—because it is. Believe, believe, and believe some more. Believe in the miracle that you are and in your own capacity to create miracles. It is your divine birthright. Trust, trust, and trust some more. Start seeing energy as it really is, knowing that everything in existence has its own unique energetic footprint. Connect with your new home and receive its love—for this is a mutual love affair. How will you generate even more love between you? Appreciate that this home has chosen you and you have chosen it. How is this going to add to your life? What new experiences will arise for you now that it's yours? How will this change your lifestyle? What will this mean for the people you love? How can you serve even more now this home has chosen you?

This approach takes belief, commitment, faith, and intent for the duration. Doubt or fear in any form voids miracles. You must get to a place of miracle strength and durability. Start small if this suits you better and gradually flex your miracle muscles as your belief and miracle power grows. Notice and be in awe of all that you draw in to increase your self-belief and self-worth: the essential ingredients of miracles.

Love is the foundation for all miracles: love of self and love of life at all times. It is the work of a lifetime but will change the entirety of your life. Life can become a platform for miracles. Give yourself permission to receive—the more grandiose miracles the better! We need to be in this energy, this mindset of miracles 24/7. This is created within from the inner space of love and peace.

If you want true love, become the love of your life first. If you want freedom, act, and feel as though you are already free. If you want great health, be grateful that your body is an amazing healer. We have to inhabit these experiences with all the accompanying thoughts and emotions into our everyday existence. It requires the best version of you every day. When you believe and behave as though your miracle is possible then you merge with your miracle. You become it; you are one with it.

Know that your power is personal with its own unique blueprint and expression of miracles. Discover what you are capable of in this lifetime. Sleep well, for it is where we work on you to work miracles.

MY IGNITION TIP

Simplify your life to meet your peace: the foundation for your love and miracles.

ILLUMINATIVE JOURNALLING INQUIRY

What is truly important to me to feel great?

Demeter
Greek Goddess

Hello, my friends. Welcome to the nurturance of you, your light and your miracles. In fact, just by absorbing the words within this light-filled book, you are engaging in deep nurturing. I wish for you to fully appreciate that if you desire to receive miracles, your own deep well needs to be full—overflowing, in fact. The reason for this is that miracles are drawn toward love, and you are the only person that can activate your ability to be and receive love. Once activated, your love becomes a magnet for miracles that are a perfect match for you and your ever-changing and evolving needs. By caring for yourself, you are teaching yourself to value yourself, respect yourself and ultimately love yourself.

Over-giving to the detriment of yourself is how you avoid being present with yourself. Over-giving can subvert or even shut down the claiming of your power as you have minimal trust in accessing and utilising your power as you have directed it to people and situations you have deemed more worthy than you. Your attention and powerful energy have been taken away from you and your needs.

Your power has been within you all along. You will only learn to trust yourself enough to receive your power when your nervous system and self-worth deem that it is safe to do so and that you are worthy. This occurs through consistent, nurturing self-care that enhances your wellbeing throughout all the cycles and seasons within your days.

Loose boundaries created by low worth and the consequent ineffectual acknowledgement of personal self-care needs can create holes that allow miracles to pass right through you without becoming yours.

ILLUMINATIVE JOURNALLING INQUIRY

What forms of self-care would most nurture me and my nervous system?

Dragons

Since the beginning of time, we have watched over your world. You may have glimpsed us in the clouds from time to time, experienced a passing memory, or had awareness in the periphery of your soul.

We are drawing close now during these times of change and rising consciousness to help you remember your greatness and to use your talents, abilities and personal attributes to create a better world for yourselves and for those to come.

We watch with eagerness as you open your hearts to move love, light and possibility. We find joy in watching you create and receive your miracles. You have been very patient in waiting for the age of miracles to become a reality—your reality.

Many of you already perceive the support that we are giving you. Ask and we are there to imbue the guidance and strength for you to burn free of old and redundant states of limitation. Allow us to assist your alchemising process: transmuting pain into wisdom and limitation into greatness.

Dragon energy is pure, ancient and powerful, and given freely to those who are here to serve and make changes within and for the development of all.

Call to us when you feel blocked and desire to ignite more of your light.

Call to us when you wish to open to more of you and your potential.

Call to us when faced with insurmountable odds.

Call to us when you have momentarily lost your way.

Call to us when you wish to break free of your current circumstances.

Call to us when you have so much to offer but don't know where to begin.

Call to us when you need a friend.

We will hear and heed your call.

We will gift to you our knowledge, insight and strength to move you forward gently and easily. Remember power is most effective when it is gentle and subtle, not forceful. Our power is available to all who stand in the light, for the light.

Allow yourself to receive insight into our world through the many myths, legends, and stories we have infused into your world. There is much healing and awakening for you to receive through our stories. Let the truth speak to you, comfort you and set you free.

MY IGNITION TIP

Open yourself to greater possibilities. Let go of what you thought was real, to embrace the 'unreal' and unseen realms. There is much to unlearn and much to learn. Embrace the excitement of knowing there is so much more to life, other dimensions and the universe than we ever imagined. Open up to more. Open up to more of you.

ILLUMINATIVE
JOURNALLING INQUIRY

Where and to what have I closed my mind
and awareness?
What new awareness can I receive this day to
open up to more of me and my gifts?

✴

El Morya
Ascended Master

Future Earth is beckoning. A new era is dawning for the betterment of mankind. Gone will be the days of darkness and despair. Love and light will prevail and carry us to new ways of being, seeing and functioning.

Light boards will exist on Earth to oversee our potential. These governing bodies will work to ensure peace and advancement towards love and its creative potential on a world scale.

Crops will be infused with the energy required to help us flourish. Our bodies will become self-healing and self-regulating. Drugs will no longer be required or desired. Psychic surgery will be common practice.

We will hear the voice of nature. Many will be able to communicate with plants and animals.

Protecting our energy and connecting with higher source frequencies are essential ingredients for miracles. To be effective miracle workers we need to protect and enhance our own energy by connecting with our higher power; this combination means your miracles are magnified. Stay in your presence and power by loving yourself and keeping strong boundaries in place indicating what is right and light for you. Your power is the foundation for miracles.

My Ignition Tip

I wonder what light boards for accelerating our
progress would look like and be like?
What can you envisage? Creating them starts
with imagining them.

Illuminative
Journalling Inquiry

What is required of me to protect and best utilise
my precious energy, my life force?

Emily Bronte
Novelist & Poet

Use your creative zone of genius to change the world. Each contribution counts, both large and small. You are serving yourself and the world every time you create. If only one person (including you) is moved by or changed in some small way then your creation is valuable. Creation fuels miracles and makes the world turn. Creation is fun and adventurous. Miracles are drawn to your love of life— your light.

Creativity is your birthright. You came from a prolific creative source. Create.

Your creative spark is linked to your love. The more you love yourself and your life, the more inspiration will arise within you and with greater regularity.

Your personal, almost inexplicably unique version of creativity is a part of your power to manifest miracles. Nurture yourself and your creativity for your best living.

Creativity and inspiration bring us alive, connecting us with our true essence.

Creativity releases from within us what we came here to express. It is cathartic, healing and uplifting on many levels. Create to fully live.

Find that part of you that contains many gifts, talents and abilities. Often the clues to your future creative success are found within what comes so easily and effortlessly to you (held within that innate part of you), and therefore perhaps not as easily identified by you as a gift. In fact, many are in awe of what we create with such ease. Step back and acknowledge your talents for them to flourish within you and show up as miracles in your day-to-day living.

First and foremost, create for yourself without regard for how your creations will be received: this will limit your creative potential. Your unfolding journey is for you and if others benefit then that is an unexpected gift to humanity.

MY IGNITION TIP

Avoid shaming your creativity with doubts about the quality of what you achieve or produce. Our creativity is like any muscle, it gets stronger with use.

ILLUMINATIVE JOURNALLING INQUIRY

What creative force and expression of my creativity is waiting to burst forth?

Eostre
Germanic Goddess

Every day is a gift of new beginnings. As each new day dawns, embrace the potential for new miracles.

Refresh, renew, reacquaint and recreate.

Live each day knowing you receive a beautiful clean slate, a redo and a fresh palette to use to create anew. Second, third and fourth chances abound. Seize each and every opportunity in each and every day. Each day counts, your best life matters. You are worthy of ever-evolving and new miracles.

Allow the energy of Spring blooming to permeate all your days. What would you like to flourish in your life today? What can you nurture? Where will you spend your precious energy for a great purpose?

Each new day is a day of new possibilities. Embrace the wonder in each day. Avoid ingratitude as it depletes your miracle power. Let your light be nourished by the sun, by nature and by all manner of experiences and beings that light you up.

As each new day begins, be a beginner in life. Learning and fresh awareness inspire us to be more and to show up more for our life. Tomorrow no longer exists and needn't define your present. What can you learn, be and accomplish today for your highest good? Love yourself and all that occurs, for you have chosen it, drawn it into your reality from your very being. The path to anything that you consider to be a miracle originates within you. Being the most spectacular 'you' creates the most uniquely designed miracles.

MY IGNITION TIP

Have a beginner mind. Be open. Be curious.
Be brand new every day. Be inspired and be an
inspiration.

ILLUMINATIVE
JOURNALLING INQUIRY

How can I break repetitive patterns this day?
What newness or fresh approach would ignite my
light this day?

Epona
Celtic Goddess

Self-worth is the miracle you require most right now. Your worth governs what you will or will not allow into your life and it speaks to you of your deservedness and governs your potential for receiving.

Find your self-worth in nature. Nature will never judge you and will move your thoughts and feelings away from self-judgement. You will find the truth of your most beautiful nature whilst communing with nature. You are a being of Earth, and you are of her nature. Remember your roots and allow for your highest potential growth. You are worthy of blooming.

Foster your deep worth by associating with those beings that see you and love your exquisite unique light. This will encourage you to feel your own worth and to express it. Many of you fear other beings and their reactions to you more than you value your own peace, love and worth. No one is worth the diminishment of you, ever. You don't enjoy spending your time in a toxic rubbish dump so avoid spending your time with people that are toxic to you.

Connect with your self-worth through a love affair with your animals. They love you unconditionally and teach you how to feel your own love. Ride with the horses, snuggle with puppies and speak with the birds. Find the animals that are for you and enjoy opening to the potential miracles within you through their love.

The strength of our self-worth either attracts or repels our miracles and energetically indicates how others should treat us, furthering impacting our worth. Honour what you require for your self-worth to flourish and invite in your miracles. Nature will soothe you back to peace and invite in your love and self-worth.
Make nature an integral part of your self-care regime.

ILLUMINATIVE
JOURNALLING INQUIRY

What thought adjustments do I require to enhance my self-worth?
What actions can I take to activate my highest self-worth?

Erebus
Greek God

Without darkness, there can be no light. Darkness allows us to see light, know light and cherish light. We see and reach for the stars as darkness descends. Life is drawn, created, and moved through contrast. Embrace darkness for it is not to be feared. To be the greatest light often periods of darkness are required.

Those who invoke miracles have arisen from their own darkness. Face any shadow aspects that are obscuring your light. Allow darkness to be your teacher, as it will assist you in letting go of what is in the way of returning you to your brightest light. Dark and light have value... they are just different, with dark being the catalyst for the light. Light creates joy and miracles just through its very existence, so we want to spend most of our time in the light.

Each individual contains both dark and light within. The Earth curriculum requires both, and there is no need to avoid the darkness as it is a highly fertile void. There is rest, there is peace, there is wisdom, there is potential in the darkness. Allow darkness and its powerful extreme, 'the dark night of the soul' to teach you, to show you all that you have put in the way of your own light. Only you are powerful enough to put in place what will conceal your light.

The underworld is not a destination, it is a place you create within through not seeking and being light in all its forms: joy, love, freedom, abundance, choice, kindness, compassion, forgiveness, inspiration, hope, faith and optimism.

You are also the only one, as per the theme of this book,

to ignite your light and unleash miracles, for yourself and others. Miracles arise through activating the highest light frequencies within for as much Earth time as possible. Face your darkness to feel your brightest light.

MY IGNITION TIP

Consider the darkness as also being a safe place, a cocoon, a retreat, a place of inner growth for outward miracles

ILLUMINATIVE JOURNALLING INQUIRY

How am I being called to retreat, restore and reflect right now?

Eva
Inner Earth Mystic

Close to you, dear Earth dwellers, is a dimension that can gift you much ancient wisdom and codes to new elevated living: Inner Earth.

Inner Earth provides balance in all things and contains the secrets of Earth and all her history. We absorb what is harmful from Earth, alchemising for beauty and replenishing what is lost. Inner Earth invites you to connect with her power to activate your own. She will fill you with the energy of light, love and inspiration, assisting you to unlock your own deep wisdom. Ask Inner Earth for the wisdom and energetic transmissions that you require to be a miracle for all of your living. Inner Earth energy will connect you with beauty and healing. Perceiving beauty and feeling beautiful and uplifted heals you and your body.

Close your eyes and travel to the centre of Inner Earth. What abundance of beauty within nature can you see, absorb and use to activate your healing? Earth and all her bodies need to be well to feel and be miraculous. Release toxicity. A healed body makes your miracle-inducing power easier to activate and house.

Open your sight, your true sight, your ability to see into other dimensions. Can you see our exquisite flowers, our cerulean lakes and gentle white waterfalls cascading over crystalline rock structures? Can you receive the depth of colour in our world and use this to open to more colour in your world: this would be a great miracle. Your eyes are a miracle and capable of seeing so much more. The beauty of natural surroundings is your portal to the energy of miracles. Allow the energy and beauty of Inner Earth to infuse your cells. Ask to see heaven in a flower, in a leaf, in a rock pool.

Come alive to all of you and the possibility that was seeded within you long ago. Connect your roots into our centre and become one with us. We welcome you, inviting you to bring Inner Earth energy to your Earth. Allow the Inner Earth energies to light the light within you. What will you do and be with your light? Where will you bestow the miracle of beauty, healing and sight? Open your capacity to see.

MY IGNITION TIP

Ask your guides to assist you to connect with Inner Earth and see in new ways: to see what you've been unwilling or unable to see.
Try my practice of releasing your ancestral emotional DNA into Inner Earth, she's a willing container to receive it and transmute it. You've held onto it and carried it for long enough. Be free to be, setting those free who come after you in your lineage. Life-changing, miracle-inducing.

ILLUMINATIVE JOURNALLING INQUIRY

What Inner Earth energies can I open to that will heal me and transform me in body, mind and spirit?

Fae
Ancient Ones

Are you ready to connect with a magical parallel world? Magic (the process) and miracles (the evidence) are interwoven; both are quite simply for bringing what you most desire into reality with the greatest of ease and for your greatest evolution.

Individuals who can perceive and receive the sacred within all things unlock magic and move into becoming the magic of themselves. Magic is drawn to magic.

What would you have to be and receive to become the most magical version of you?

Would it be loving yourself consistently to engage your inner magic?

Would it be raising your frequency to receive our world?

Would it be being in this world but not of it, knowing there is more than you currently perceive?

Would it be opening your eyes and vision to see into other dimensions?

Would it be remembering your Avalonian or Celtic origins?

Would it be connecting with ancient Druid wisdom?

Open, open, open. Open to more. More possibility, more of you.

Let new wisdom subtly and effortlessly start to infiltrate your being—you must ask for it as you live in a free-will world.

Stepping into magic allows life to flow with ease and there is no difficulty in bringing what you desire for your highest good into your reality.

As you open to your own sacred, the sacred will be

drawn to you. Nature is a portal into the magical world of the fae. You can learn much from our world and how we create if you open your heart, mind and awareness beyond three-dimensional living. Sit quietly and ask to travel energetically to our dimension and you may just be granted entry if we decide you are worthy (loving) and Earth will benefit. We are all about reciprocity, a mutual exchange for the benefit of all. Gifts are to be shared, to help us all evolve into our next level: a unique requirement for every being.

Connect with all the signs, symbols and messages we send you to assist you to find our magic and yours. We will enjoy weaving our beautiful world with yours.

You will know our world is merging with yours when you see more consciousness, light, love and miracles filtering into your archaic patriarchal political systems; advances in food sourcing and distribution; more widespread life-enhancing infrastructure; changes in definitions of work to support living; more telepathic communication and more conscious approaches to healing and wellbeing. Your 'world' will feel lighter with more emphasis on play. There will be greater ease in accessing your innate wisdom and it will become a natural way of relating to yourself and life. You will enjoy your magic, share your gifts, embrace the sacred, and learn to receive natural beauty and wonder as a daily approach to best living.

MY IGNITION TIP

Read stories of the fae to reacquaint yourself with this magical dimension, there is much truth in fantasy. Reading these stories can invoke some ancient knowledge.

ILLUMINATING JOURNALLING INQUIRY

What special talents, gifts and abilities do you possess that the fae could assist you to activate? It is an ask and receive universe.

Freya
Norse Goddess

In any battle, there is a point where things change. That time is now. You have all waged a great war against the limitations of unconsciousness. Your efforts are bringing miraculous change. Have faith in you and your fellow Earth companions for many are being incredible and doing incredible things. Take a moment to celebrate the many victories both small and large that are occurring within you and throughout the world at this time.

Remember to focus your energy on what is working as it is too easy to become overwhelmed by the challenges that are presented. Be grateful and honour the good to raise the light.

Many of you are tired and feel like retreating. Keep going, for there are many miracles to be received and enjoyed for your efforts on the other side of these turbulent times. Find your eye in the storm whenever you can. Rest is required as much as action, otherwise, your miracles will be void of fuel. Raise your light by retreating when necessary. Restorative times are vital for your health, wellbeing and for the optimal strength that life is calling to you to garner and demonstrate.

Choose your future battles wisely. What can you surrender to and flow with? Not every battle is yours. Each person has their own work to do and often you need to withdraw, regroup, concede and just heal yourself. Don't lose yourself in this world. Remember, you are ultimately a spiritual being having an earthly life and everyone has their part to play. It is a team effort. Seek support as often as you can. The world needs the best, most nourished version of you for performing the miracles needed during these times.

Thank you for being here to usher in a new era. I honour all that you are and all that you are becoming. The part you are playing in the evolution of life here is miraculous. Unleash the greatest you.

My Ignition Tip

Give yourself permission to care for yourself first and foremost. The work that is calling to you cannot be miraculous if you are not replenished and vital. Your self-care is calling to you. Your higher purpose requires and desires your commitment to self-care.

Illuminative Journalling Inquiry

What self-care is calling to me most during this time?

Gaia
Goddess of Earth

We are nature. Remember your true nature and ground into your roots. Our physical and emotional bodies are nourished by all of nature. To be a conduit for miracles and an expression of miracles the physical and emotional bodies need to be in harmony. Be present in your body; it is your physical vehicle for the conscious manifestation of miracles. Inner peace is activated most effectively through nature. Find your peace, your place in nature. Tune into your innermost desires for nature:

Is it a snowy vista you require?

Is it an ocean plunge?

Is it the crystal-clear reflections of a lake?

Is it sunshine on your skin?

Is it getting your hands into soil?

Is it the beauty of flowers?

Is it a rainforest walk?

Is it waterfalls and churning white water?

Is it walking in the cleansing rain?

Is it receiving the hope and blessings of a rainbow?

Is it a desire to connect with the earth elementals?

Is it crystals that are calling to you?

Do you need to plant some seeds and tend to them?

The most grounded, stable, nourished and elevated version of you is most essential for accessing your miraculous nature and the associated miracle effect. Being the best version of yourself is your catalyst for miracles.

Regularly walk barefoot and ground your energies deep into Mother Earth or hold a tree and ask for her to ground your energies into the earth. Nature requires nourishment and balance in all things as do you. If one element is missing, blooming (your miracles) is impacted. Tend to yourself as you would tend to the most beautiful garden. Ground your energies, ground into your life. A strong foundation is needed to support yourself and your propensity for miracles. Connect with nature as your base, your platform for miracles. Nature is abundant in miracles and does not resist them or place limits on them. Nature does not resist her greatness. To be miraculous, one must receive their greatness, not hide from it. Nature is willing to amaze and dazzle at any moment. She also knows there is power in stillness and quiet receptivity. Tuning into yourself and your needs allows you to embrace your strength and ability to readily manifest miracles. Nature is willing to flourish in the most obscure locations and under the most challenging conditions—just as you can. Flow with nature and all of life. Allow your miracles to be at one with you and all of life, connected to the ebbs and flows and cycles and seasons.

MY IGNITION TIP

Witness miracles in nature as a starting
point for observing them and attracting them
into your own life.

ILLUMINATIVE
JOURNALLING INQUIRY

What wisdom and analogies for life can you
receive from nature?

Green Tara
Buddhist Goddess of Wisdom & Compassion

Green Tara wants us to know that we are coming to an end of a cycle. Wanting and craving and domination over others will be replaced with self-autonomy, inner sanctuary and peace. Our power will serve ourselves and others through love. The old conditions will fall away, making way for a new dawn. Green Tara encourages us to embrace grace. There is great power in grace, it is calm, inspiring, and based on love of self and respect for others. Grace invokes majestic beauty, deeply connecting with one's own love and peace and radiating that outward. Grace touches others, connecting them with their own inner light and love. Grace is flowing with all of life. Grace knows effortless miracles; they naturally flow to her as they love and respect her. As with miracles, her peace and worth know no bounds. Embrace your grace.

MY IGNITION TIP

Embrace your grace to ease your suffering and connect you with your love. Enjoy how life responds to this calm, elegant and peaceful version of you.

ILLUMINATIVE JOURNALLING INQUIRY

In what ways can I connect with and
express my grace?

Gula
Mesopotamian
Goddess of Healing

Many of you right now are running on empty. You have forgotten the delicate balance between act and flow and between your own self-care requirements and service.

Your miracles require the most nourished and powerful version of you. Tune into your self-care needs at this time. Build moments of self-care into all your days to counteract and support the pace of your life and the spiritual growth that you are undertaking. Spiritual growth is essential to ignite your light and unleash your miracles. Be aware of how taxing this uplevelling is on your body. Your body requires constant recalibration to house your increasing light. The pace of your evolution has never before been so great, therefore, the requirement for balance in all things and devotion to yourself through self-care is of utmost importance in supporting your new way of being. Self-care and personal growth have a symbiotic relationship, and both are essential for the ultimate endgame: creating, receiving and being a miracle.

Educate yourself with nature's pharmacy. There is great untapped potential here. A remedy exists in nature for all that ails and there are phenomenal healers with great knowledge and skill in this area.

MY IGNITION TIP

Allow healthy organic food and herbs to become your medicine. If you are in a position to do so, educate others. Awareness of consumption is essential for optimal health. Reconnect with your ancient wisdom. Remember the old ways for healing and enhanced wellbeing.

ILLUMINATIVE JOURNALLING INQUIRY

What does my body most require and desire for healing today?

Hecate
Greek Goddess
of Magic

You have magic pulsing through your veins. For now, it may be just a little glimmer, a little tingle, an invitation to receive what is to come.

You are in between worlds at this time, which can be confusing and uncomfortable, but at the same time, hope and curiosity are alive within you, drawing you towards the miraculous potential of you.

Learn to feel magic all around you. If you sense magic, you will learn to see and activate magic.

Feel the magic in a butterfly's wings.

Feel the magic of bees pollinating.

Feel the magic of the sun's rays streaming through clouds.

Feel the magic in a hug.

Feel the magic in the birth of a new creation.

Feel the magic of new awareness, of a revelation.

Feel the magic in coincidence and synchronicity.

Feel the magic of sun on your skin.

Magic and miracles are synonymous and are yours to claim. Witness magic to receive magic, to be magic.

MY IGNITION TIP

Many have forgotten that our world is magical.
Close your eyes and use the power of your mind
and heart to imagine the most magical world.
Use all your senses and ask to draw what you see
and experience into your reality. Remember how
powerful and truly magical you are.

ILLUMINATIVE
JOURNALLING INQUIRY

What magic is in evidence for you today?
What magic can you see, feel and think into
existence?

Helen of Troy
Goddess

Dear readers,

Welcome to a new way of being on our planet. I like this new world of bright light that is emerging. New Earth has more equality and less oppression; the divine feminine is rising and creating more possibilities for love to reign. Thank you to all the powerful, aware men who are embracing the sacred masculine and, in so doing, supporting the flowering of the divine feminine. Yin and Yang is a beautiful and powerful entwinement bringing forth all that is great, wonderful and transformative. Yin and Yang can exist in all things. Embrace your Yin and Yang by being all that you are: relishing all of the complementary paradoxes within you and in all of life.

Seek your balance. Miracles are created through balance in all things. Balance brings harmony. Peace through balance is a powerful precursor to miracles as it deeply sets the stage for love. Loving more freely arises from peace.

Love exists throughout eternity, all else retreats into the background of existence. Place your energy where love is ignited to connect with your miracle strength. Find love in beauty. Beauty can be in a face that launches a thousand ships; it can be in a flower; within an ocean wave; seen in a luminescent moon; within words on a page; or within the ever-changing colours of a sunset. See your beauty and connect with it all around you. Beauty will assist you to discover the miracles within you waiting to be shared for love to flourish and elevate humankind.

MY IGNITION TIP

Take your energy to where love exists as
frequently as possible.
Open your heart to where you have always
had it closed.

ILLUMINATIVE
JOURNALLING INQUIRY:

How can I embrace the divine feminine
arising within me?
How can I embrace the divine masculine
arising within me?

Hera
Greek Goddess

Share yourself and your gifts. There is great power and miracles to generate through alliance. Powerful souls combining leads to amplified light and possibility.

Move away from a scarcity mentality. There is enough room for everyone to step into miracles that are personally unique. One person experiencing a miracle does not negate another receiving a miracle. Avoid comparing your miracles to those of others. Trust that your miracles are what you require for your highest good. They are designed perfectly for you. Create an abundance mindset for yourself and your fellow beings. There is no competition for miracles. Reaching and grabbing for all manner of things as if they need to be fought over is the ego at work. Be the energy of what you desire to receive without diminishing it by interfering with your process via self-limiting comparison and competition. Believe that you are worthy of all that you desire and gift others this same belief.

Celebrating the successes of others moves you directly into the sphere of miracles. When you acknowledge and appreciate the success of others you are showing the universe that you would like to have opportunities for celebrating your own success. You can activate your own opportunities for success by vicariously tuning into the feeling of success experienced by others. Going down the erroneous path of 'pity me, poor me, why didn't this happen for me, why does everything great happen for him or her?' is the opposite of creating a miracle space. Genuinely feeling happiness for the personal wins and achievements of others is an indicator of a higher-frequency functioning individual. Higher-frequency living draws miracles. There is more than enough wonder, love, beauty, opportunity and success for everyone. Be in alliance, resist separation. There is great power in oneness. Combine your strength and your highest frequency to create miracles of increasing magnitude.

MY IGNITION TIP

There is room for us all to be miraculous. We can create a miraculous home environment, organisation and even society through mutual respect and effort. Coming together, collaborating and supporting one another amplifies miracles.

ILLUMINATIVE JOURNALLING INQUIRY

How can you raise your frequency by genuinely feeling happy for and celebrating the success of another?

Hesperides
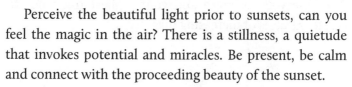
Goddess of
Sunsets

Perceive the beautiful light prior to sunsets, can you feel the magic in the air? There is a stillness, a quietude that invokes potential and miracles. Be present, be calm and connect with the proceeding beauty of the sunset.

Sunsets invite elevation to higher frequencies.

Sunsets connect you with your expansiveness.

Sunsets take you to the energy of miracles.

Sunsets take you from the mundane to the extraordinary.

Sunsets connect you with your higher self-guidance.

Sunsets are miracles reminding you of your inner ancient wisdom and of your own ability to create miracles as natural occurrences.

Viewing a sunset with many beings who are all simultaneously lit up by nature's display is a powerfully potent container for miracles. Send your miracle requests out into sunsets, allowing them to be fuelled by your heightened magic and then absorbed into the ethers.

Allow sunsets to serve as a reminder to connect with all of nature, for you are an integral part of nature. Nature loves being witnessed by you. Plants thrive when gazed upon with love. You can enhance the natural kingdom through your elevated presence. Be a miracle for nature. Earth needs you to thrive to gift to you her best. Nature serves you best when you serve her best. Reciprocal blooming is miraculous.

Realise and become your truest nature through nature. Nature calms, grounds and centres, bringing you back to the truth of you. Allow her to speak with you to assist you in remembering yourself. Become lost in nature to discover more of you. Remembering all of your nature will bring you back to your miraculous nature.

You are not your possessions.

You are not your thoughts.

You are not your emotions.

You are not your relationships.

You are not your career.

You are not your past.

You are your light, ignite it.

All of Earth desires and requires your light.

MY IGNITION TIP

Explore your own patches of nature: a flower in a vase, an insect in a plant, your garden in bloom, an entirely new vista. Witness what may have been previously unseen by you: miracles in action.

ILLUMINATIVE JOURNALLING INQUIRY

Nature reflects you, back to you.
What would nature like you to know about your nature?
What would nature like to gift to you?

Hilarion
Master Healer &
Ascended Master

I feel the malaise of many, the stagnant energy resulting from less-than-ideal health. A healed person is a more whole person and a greater vessel for miracles. Invite in your potential for healing. Ask for all those who can contribute to your healing to show up and reveal themselves to you at every opportune time. Invite in the emerald ray of healing to flood every cell of your body and to flow into your precious energy field. Protect your energies to nourish your mind, body and soul.

Wellness and vitality are the miracles you require most right now to provide fertile ground for seeding more miracles. Commit to healing all aspects of yourself: emotionally, mentally, physically and spiritually. Receive the messages of your soul through your emotions and body. Sit with your feelings, acknowledge them, learn from them and then make the choice to release them. Heal your life: body, mind and soul, and share the most whole version of you with others. In doing so, you are assisting the activation of healing within others. Each of you has your own code for healing, be willing to receive and act upon your healing wisdom. Release all limited thinking and fear; embrace the possibility of healing miracles. Belief is everything. All that you require to heal is within you and all around you. Commit to receiving your most healed, most whole self and the stars will align just for you. A healed self is needed to best serve you and others. Invite in the miracle of bringing new healing information into your life and into the world. Help the healing of the entire planet. Every person makes a difference.

MY IGNITION TIP

Heal your heart, body, and spirit to fully receive your soul gifts and the power of your love and radiant light. Awaken to your deep, ancient, sacred healing knowledge.

ILLUMINATIVE JOURNALLING INQUIRY

What do you most require for healing at this time? What knowledge of ancestral healing arts do I contain within me that I can now activate?

Horus

Egyptian God

We all come from the stars and have stardust within us. Look up, look up to the stars. Connect with the stars and celestial bodies. Look through my EYE and develop your cosmic vision. It is time to expand your awareness beyond the earthly plane to other dimensions and times, to become the expanded, cosmic version of you.

Observe the stars in the night sky and draw down their energy to unlock your star wisdom and star power. Look up, look up, look up—there is your miracle.

What will you do with your star power and star knowledge? Will you use it to free yourself of minor earthly concerns and see a bigger-picture cosmic reality?

Allow your clairvoyance to open, and to serve you and others. Remember your starry origins. We are all star seeds here today within the pages of this book, waiting to ignite our light. Feel the energy of your stardust, draw it into every cell of your body and being. Light up as the star being you truly are; be the miracle.

MY IGNITION TIP

Star gaze. Lay down under the stars. Ask questions of the stars, connect with your star origins and receive messages from your stars.
Be a shooting star.

Iris
Greek Rainbow
Goddess

As above so below...

Please know that heaven is closer to Earth than you may perceive. Have hope that it is possible to create heaven on Earth, making miracles commonplace. Miracles of all kinds are happening for many elevating the world, thus drawing heaven closer to Earth.

Individuals must break free of constrained living, branching into new endeavours, and stretching humanity beyond its current 'borders' into new paradigms, energies, and ways of working and living to elevate living to greater miraculous states. We need people to fall in love with their living and to find the work that they will love. Work that foremost serves self and others as a wonderful consequence provides fertile ground for miracles. Miracles being occurrences that invoke surprise, awe and joy in the recipient, creating beautiful energy for all who are nearby, equally blessed to witness or experience a miracle.

Look to rainbows to remind you of the magic available in life if you are willing to rise to meet it. Your pot of gold is not as elusive as you may have been conditioned to believe. What if your imagination and creativity were the only true limitations in your life? Start dreaming and imagining your miracle life into existence. Every thought and emotion counts as this combination directly influences your vibration, that is, what you are radiating out into the world and drawing towards you.

MY IGNITION TIP

Use the full power of yourself (heart, mind and spirit) to make your thinking and corresponding emotions highly positive for igniting your dreams and enticing miracles.

ILLUMINATIVE JOURNALLING INQUIRY

What is in the pot of gold at the end of my rainbow?

Isis
Egyptian Goddess

Magic is the way of the light. Access to this mysterious, wonderful, exciting phenomenon called magic is an intrinsic part of your life force. It is the truth of you. Magic is your inner light and birthright. It swirls around you and your life, waiting to land and awaken within you. It is your manifesting power; it is your miracle worker persona. It is underneath your stuff: the wounds, the untruths, the restricted points of view and the personal set of limitations. Free yourself to find the magic of you. Face it all—it is nowhere near as bad as you think as it is mainly based on illusion constructed by the ego. Set it all on fire and start anew. You never needed any of that stuff as it has kept you from love, the true source of magic.

Be the observer of your mind and emotions until you have unlocked 'you'. This is where you will use calm and inner peace as your foundation for living. From here, magic can find an opening to flow in.

I speak for magic—that place that exists within every being. It is both within the Earth and of the cosmos. The divine spark within every individual is magic waiting to bloom. Magical elements come into play when one is aligned with life purpose, higher self and source energy. Magic has been unleashed, it is eternal and available for all who are clear channels to receive it and activate it within.

Magic is freedom, freedom from the ego and shadow aspects that have had sovereignty for too long. As people awaken to the truth of themselves as light beings, filled with love and light, magic can prevail. Magic is a coming-together for all beings, seen and unseen. It is oneness.

Magic is inspired living. It is waking up each day excited about what may come, and at the same time not needing to know what may come. It is childlike excitement, surrender to mystery and wonder, and trust in life as life presents. It is seeing beauty and sensing amazement in any experience or opportunity. It is loving oneself and all of life unconditionally. It is flow and peace. It is having a thought, an idea and watching it manifest with ease if it is for the highest good of all. Magic will bring aliveness and joy and fashion your days into authentic existence. Magic is living through and with light. It is being in the world but not of it. It is operating at a greater frequency. Magic draws magic onto itself, as it creates a magnetic attraction to itself. Magic replenishes and creates simultaneously. Magic is goddess energy prevailing on Earth as it has arisen and been claimed by many. It is power unleashed in true service and magnitude. Magic is the power of hope, optimism and love. Magic is consistently elevated emotions and high vibration; it is your light ignited.

MY IGNITION TIP

Breathe and be calm. Release stress, pressure, doubt and worry, and ease into your magic instead. Remember you are a magical being with many amazing abilities. Create the space to enjoy the ignition of your magic.

ILLUMINATIVE JOURNALLING INQUIRY

Imagine you are a fantasy writer with the special gift of writing your words into reality. Write about your new magical world and your new magical life. What will you do and be with your magic? What will your magic allow you to create?

Ishtar
Babylonian Great Goddess

Life is a mystery and speaks to those who are willing to receive the power of the unseen, unknown realms through codes, symbols, images, sounds and synchronicity. To step into the space of miracles receptivity to this cosmic and earthly messaging needs to become your new normal. Look up to the heavens and at the same time be at one with Earth. Allow both realms to connect you with the power of your congruent heart and mind, to open up further to greater possibility and wonder.

Release distraction and chaos. If you are stressed, you have chosen to react to something that you've made more significant than you, thus diminishing your connection to the creative life force that is calling for you to connect with, to become one with.

Tune into the flood of prevalent signs and messages that have been created just for you to lead you along the path of miracles. The possibility of a miracle (or many) is always there for you. Your task in this lifetime is to elevate yourself and your energetic frequency. Move to the frequency of love, peace and faith, as this is where your miracles arise. Rise up to meet them. You know how, this potential has been within you all along. Release the fight to stay small and connected to the lower workings of the mind. Your best life demands that you align your mind with your most loving and powerful heart, opening you up to the miraculous infinite potential of the universe. You exist beyond this world, beyond this time and space. Embrace this truth to know more of yourself and to open your gateway to miracles.

MY IGNITION TIP

Release control of trying to keep your world small and familiar. Step into the unknown invisible realms to meet the (as yet) unknown miraculous aspects of you. There is so much wonder and joy in discovery to be experienced.

ILLUMINATIVE JOURNALLING INQUIRY

What is deep within me that I can now meet with great receptivity?

Jesus of Nazareth

Honour thy fellow man as all are equal and all have gifts to share. Gifts for the service of mankind are actualised after darkness is confronted and healed. Light brings the potential for much, including miracles. Miracles change paradigms and create a higher frequency to live in. This is what all humankind is seeking, even if not all know this yet. The wheel is turning slowly, but it is turning. Each small shift will be felt in the hearts and minds of many, stimulating change and gaining momentum as more awaken to the truth of themselves.

There is no longer a need for suffering and sacrifice to be your primary modes of learning. Open your hearts to see and find your truth and purpose through love, joy, service and contribution, all of which are miraculous vehicles for transformation.

In time, you will come to know that faith (not fear) is the great facilitator behind the orchestration of your miracles.

'Truly I tell you, if you have faith as small as a mustard seed, you can say this to the mountain, "Move from here to there," and it will move. Nothing will be impossible for you.'
Matthew 17:20-21

My Ignition Tip

Find your gifts of service: life-changing and joy-creating for you and others.

Illuminative Journalling Inquiry

Where have I made myself better than another?
Where have I made myself less than another?
Where can I step into the middle ground of
honouring myself and others simultaneously?

Joan of Arc
Patron Saint
& Leader

Your bravery is your miracle. This sentence is so important for you to embrace that it must be repeated again and again. **Your bravery is your miracle.** Say it with me now, 'My bravery is my miracle.'

Unless it is used as a guide to show you what controls you, not as a predeterminer of your choices, actions and destiny, your fear is your foe. Slay your fear daily by whatever means you can access within you and all around you for this purpose. Draw on the very depths of your being. Connect with your power from all lifetimes and jump into the future to access it there. Your power and strength are everywhere and in everything so long as you stop fighting so hard to stay small, scared and limited. Your smallness is a myth—your myth.

Receive the truth of your magnificence. You must fight for this, for you, this lifetime. Your freedom, your greatest miracle, is on the other side of your fear. Surround yourself with those that bring healing, light, love and wholeness to your life. Let go of the rest as you have placed them in your life to keep you safe and small. Release them and meet your new team—those that will help you ignite your light and unleash you, the miracle of you.

Love your fear away, laugh at it, smile (even smirk) in the face of it, and as per the title of this book, ignite it with your light. Your fear cannot win you if you desire a miraculous, expansive life. It is not real, and it never was. Know this within your heart, mind and body.

Your miracles require your belief in yourself and your dreams. Believing in yourself requires relentless bravery.

Miracles arise from feelings of worth. Worth is elevated when you reach your upper limits and stretch some more, always extending the boundaries of you and your life to your extreme. Achieve this by increments, one 'stretch' and one 'reach' at a time. This needs to become your natural default system, the way you live your life, not something that occurs only on a feel-good, inspired day. If you desire miracles, you require (from yourself) the choice to create and live a very expanded life. Contracting, shrinking and detouring in the face of fear is not an invitation for miracles. Stand in your truth and express it and live it fearlessly. Be the defender of your freedom, your voice and your power.

Stand tall in your presence, for it is great, far greater than you can imagine. Stretch, grow and become unstoppable, then you will meet your power and miraculous nature. Rise up and rise again. Free yourself from the shackles of illusion, removing all veils obscuring your true sight and extraordinary awareness. There is your unleashed miracle: the greatness of you and the invincible way you work your light for yourself and others. You will change your world and be a great contributor to the evolution of the whole: for oneness and for universal, infinite, creative potential.

MY IGNITION TIP

Acknowledge your bravery. Honour your journey.
Look back over your life and appreciate all that you
have overcome. We are all great warriors for light
in these times. Each time you claim more of you,
you are changing your ancestral lineage. We can be
all those things our ancestors were not capable of
being or choosing.

ILLUMINATIVE JOURNALLING INQUIRY

What bravery have I shown in my lifetime
that I can celebrate today?

Juliet Capulet
Love Goddess

Capture the power of your desire for drawing to you a love like no other. Life is for loving and sharing and expressing that love. Write your destiny love story in the stars. You are worthy of great love: a true and life-long enduring miracle. Seek your great love by being your own great love. Love yourself like you would your greatest love. It is easier to attract what you already are. Be magnetic to great love.

Love is always worth any perceived risk. Love is never a risk to the heart, only to the ego. The ego likes a contained, safe and often predictable love affair. Make your love story the stuff of legends.

It is better to have loved with great depth and passion (even if only for a fleeting time) than to never have experienced it at all. The truest love can never be extinguished or lost as it exists across all of time. You can love whenever, whatever and whomever you choose, even if only from afar. There is no limit to who and what we can love. Make all your love miraculous: be a living, loving miracle.

MY IGNITION TIP

Stay open to possibilities beyond what life has told us is truth. History is always open to interpretation. There are many truths within so-called untruths. When Juliet 'arrived' for channelling, I initially hesitated as I had always believed her to be a 'fictional' character, although deep down I had sensed a greater truth. When I did some research and typed in, 'Was Juliet a real person?' my screen flashed in quick succession over 50 times on the words, 'Juliet was a real person', It was quite surreal and made me wonder if many so-called fictional stories in our time are steeped in truth. Believe in the impossible even if it is not a popular, dominant opinion. There is magic in quiet truths.

ILLUMINATIVE JOURNALLING INQUIRY

What greater truths can I open my heart and mind to receive—to be revealed for me this day?

Julius Caesar
Warrior & Creator

The only battle that should be waged is with the self. Winning the battle over fear and limitation will keep many busy for much of their lifetime: the greatest, most transformative conquering of all. The world will transform, allowing peace to prevail when man overcomes himself, embracing his true greatness. Many beautiful women are already leading the way: bow to them, honour them, respect them. The character of a man is reflected in the way he treats the women in his world. Treat them well and they will be magic and create miracles for you and others. Suppress your women and you will suppress yourself and your best living. Women are flowers, nourish them well and watch them bloom.

Use your energy and power to leave a great legacy behind: a legacy of creation, abundance, freedom, power and love for life. Envision, imagine and create the world you would like to inhabit right into your existence. No other being can create this desired life or provide it for you. Remember why you have chosen to be here at this time.

Be an active participant in all of life. Spread the parameters of what you believe is truly possible if you desire miracles. Miracles are on mute without belief and are only barely received by the universe. Step into your power (the best version of yourself) to fire up your potential for miracles: receiving and honouring those grand, pivotal moments in life, those appearing unexpectedly or just when you most require them. Life is magical for those who believe it to be so.

MY IGNITION TIP

Love your new life and a new world into being
with miraculous intention as fuel.

ILLUMINATIVE
JOURNALLING INQUIRY

What dream can I now activate that I had always
considered impossible?

Kali
Hindu Goddess

Face your darkness—that is, all that you have put in place via your thoughts, beliefs, words, conditioning and actions—to release your light, your firepower.

Your miracles require your fearlessness because anything you fear is not the truth of you, nor the essence of you, but rather a dimmed down, compartmentalised, limited version of you.

Own the fact that you are the only one capable of stopping you. All that you are is all that you have decided to believe and evolve into based on what you have observed and experienced in life. Now is the time to release your past to claim the power of now and the possibility of the future. You have often followed the known, yet limited path. Now that you have built your awareness and embraced your light, it is your time to tread the path of the unknown to find your new potential and possibilities.

With your hand on your heart, say and believe:

'I release all that does not serve me in being the whole truth of who I am.'

'I release all that I have placed in the way of me activating my light and achieving all that I came here to do and create.'

Break down the ties to your ego, it is designed to keep you in the dark, obscured from your light. You are free, you are safe; you no longer require this archaic 'safety' mechanism. It is obsolete.

Your cave of darkness will shift to one of light when you free yourself from the power that people-pleasing has over you. You were born to be different, to stand out from the crowd, to be all of you. You are not here to please others or make anyone proud of you. For a time, it may only be you, for you. Be you and your true tribe will come... they are awaiting your light to guide them towards you, to recognise you. Be a strong beacon for others. Always remember that your miracles arise from your light, not your darkness.

MY IGNITION TIP

Are you sensing how powerful we truly are? It's time to wipe our slates clean and breathe life into a new canvas—one that aligns with all that we love, cherish and desire for our highest good.

ILLUMINATIVE JOURNALLING INQUIRY

Make a list of all your perceived limitations. Now, cross each one out and turn the limitation into a strength by turning them into positive 'I am' statements.

Kuthumi
Ascended Master

Embrace energy healing work to unlock, access and activate your ancient soul gifts and deep wisdom. Third-eye activation, clearing and balancing is your portal for receiving the ancient wisdom that is encoded within you. Now is the time for receiving your unique blueprint: your innate gifts and the necessary wisdom for advancing your purpose and pathway throughout this life. Moving forward with your ancient wisdom is the requirement for effectively serving you and others in heightened ways. This is for the betterment of all. Raising the frequency of the planet as a whole and understanding that all beings are connected and that what enhances ONE contributes to the whole are vital concepts to embrace in moving humanity forward. Enough individuals seeking this way of being elevates those who still cannot fully be the greatness of themselves at this time. Your sight helps to awaken those who cannot yet fully see. Wisdom combined with light and love forges great miracles.

Energy healing bypasses the mind, circumventing any blocks to receiving soul gifts and third-eye vision. Energy work raises one's vibration to receive all that once seemed impossible. It connects every individual to the higher self and to the cosmic field of love and infinite potential.

Energy healing allows us to move away from our human selves and closer to our divine selves. Your ancient wisdom and soul gifts are the miracles you have been waiting for. You can see clearly now.

MY IGNITION TIP

In raising our own awareness and vibration we are indirectly assisting those around us. Acknowledge the work that you are doing on yourself that is contributing to the betterment of the whole.

ILLUMINATIVE JOURNALLING INQUIRY

In what ways am I more connected to others than I previously realised?
How can I use this understanding to open up to even more of myself?

Lady Nada
Ascended Master

Love is your miracle, be it and express it everywhere you can in every way you can. Place love at the forefront of life rather than just something you reflect on in good times. Love can exist in every situation, no matter how difficult or uncomfortable. Grief, loss and discomfort of any kind can be transmuted into something different and greater through connecting with the love within as well as the cosmic field of infinite love—much power is generated when the two are activated simultaneously. Making the decision with intent and commitment to be and receive love will be the most life-changing choice of your lifetime. Love allows new paradigms and new ways of perceiving all of life, and allows the mundane to be elevated to the space of miracles. Learn to connect with love through the simplest of elements and moments. Love can be found within the unfolding petals of a rose as equally as it can be discovered within another being. Love is not discerning or selective, it is omnipresent. You are love in seed, bud and bloom.

MY IGNITION TIP

Be an expression of an aspect of love every day.
Will you choose kindness, compassion, gratitude,
optimism, hope, excitement, nurturing, tolerance,
enthusiasm, forgiveness, self-care, service
or peace today?

ILLUMINATIVE
JOURNALLING INQUIRY

Where can I receive love today that may have been
previously unobserved or unappreciated by me?

Lady Portia
Ascended Master

Power born of light to fuel change is what is needed on our planet. Many individuals have successfully completed several cosmic lessons and absolved karma.

It is your mission to heal and learn from your own karma and allow others to complete their own curriculum. Karma is a gift to humanity and should never be seen as something that is inflicted. Karma is of the light and occurs through love. It provides a record of growth and indicates what a soul requires next on the journey of evolution and enlightenment. Dharma is achieved when the karma of this lifetime is released, and dharma is the activation of destiny and soul missions for the greater good, both individually and collectively. Individuals can then step into the magnificence of their true light, unobscured by past learning or functioning. This light gives rise to miracles of all kinds, raising the vibration of the planet. Earth can become a planet of miracles if a great proportion of the population embraces the full degree of their expansive light-fuelled power. Stay present and receive in totality all that life is orchestrating for your own healing and the great movement towards ascension to higher levels of being.

MY IGNITION TIP

Surrender to the grand plan for you and your life.
Resistance is futile and delays our progress. Much
is in place to help us release karma and move into
dharma. Accept what is, anticipate the best, take
on board the learning and messages, make amends
where necessary and release what no longer serves.

ILLUMINATIVE
JOURNALLING INQUIRY

Which karmic lessons am I currently working on?
How can I move through this stage in the shortest
possible timeframe with a foundation of
grace and love?

Lady Venus
Ascended Master

Connecting with your own heart is your portal to divine love and to understanding the miracle of you. Learn to honour and understand your own connection to universal source energy via your experience of the love within you. Listen and learn but ultimately feel into what resonates with you. Only you can intuit what is required for you. Surrender to the experiences that are designed to bring you closer to love.

You will come to understand your own unique connection with love and your personal expression of love when you value love—and commit to it more fully—more so than you focus on fear. Love and miracles require action, they require you to show up fully for yourself and all of life. Fear allows for passivity, victimhood and immovability. Seek the message that is underneath the fear to find your freedom from it.

Enhancing your self-worth is your first miracle assignment. Until you value yourself, the rest of the world does not get the message. Your ability to receive miracles is directly influenced by your level of deservedness and worthiness. Low self-worth has the potential to push love and miracles away. Being a person who functions from love draws miraculous moments into your energy field. Know you are valuable and worthy at all times (without exception and in all circumstances) to build your capacity for drawing miracles towards you.

Secondly, treat all beings with respect. They may not be experiencing life as you are; each individual has their own challenges to face and wisdom to gain. Many are doing enough right now to just survive their current circumstances. Have compassion for the journeys of others.

Thirdly, and perhaps most importantly, love everything that shows up in your life, for it is your divine teacher. Recognise that all of life conspires to bring you closer to wholeness every moment of every day. Resist nothing, embrace everything—this is the miraculous stance you have been waiting for.

Open to more love, to more of you. Your miracles can then reach a magnitude that has previously eluded you and been concealed from those who would benefit from your highest frequency and manifestation power. Rather than just thinking about what you would like to manifest, you can be the source of bringing your aspirations out of your mind and into your miraculous reality for a new age.

MY IGNITION TIP

Do a judgement inventory. Look at how respect can replace disrespect.

ILLUMINATIVE JOURNALLING INQUIRY

What limiting beliefs and stories can I release from my mind to allow me to feel more into my heart space, my love and my worth?

Lakshmi
Hindu Goddess
of Fortune

Be the fortunate one while knowing that a fortune is not a prerequisite. All riches arise within and then materialise in your world taking various forms.

Seek your light to find your fortune and your most fortunate life.

Your fortune will be found in your wisdom.

Your fortune will be found in expressions of your beauty.

Your fortune will be found in your love.

Your fortune will be found in your purpose and its ensuing fortune.

Your fortune will be found in your peace and joy.

Enjoy a fortune of success, love, joy and abundance. What will you choose? Know that all manner of fortunate miracles are yours.

Your miracles will arise from the fortune you possess within. Be fortunate. Share your good fortune with others and enjoy how it multiplies and transforms into something awe-inspiring and worthy of celebration.

MY IGNITION TIP

Connect with your beautiful light. Allow this radiant light to illuminate your path to riches and miracles of all kinds.

ILLUMINATIVE JOURNALLING INQUIRY

What fortunes are already within me and
showing up in my life?

Leizi
Chinese Goddess

Life is a living miracle when it becomes a revelation. A revelation is an opening to something undiscovered, unexperienced, or unknown. You came to Earth, dear miracle worker, to reveal yourself to you. Each moment of awareness predisposes you to the potential of a life-enhancing revelation. Embrace your revelations with love; there is nothing to fear and freedom and light to gain.

Revelations are life-changing because through them you receive more of you to carry you through life. The revelatory you is the greatest you. Most individuals function from a small percentage of their true capacity. This state is not entirely due to personal 'fault' since this is how society is set up: conform to the majority; follow the desired programs and protocols; defer control to those in authority; get someone else to fix your physical and emotional health; don't trust yourself as you might fail; stay small, limited and safe; forget you are a spiritual being having an earthly experience; and above all else, don't believe in magic, miracles and infinite possibilities. This cultural conditioning all contributes to the diminishment of society rather than to its advancement. Unfortunately, it also leaves power in the hands of a few, a few that may not be the best for global change and advancement on a spiritual and evolutionary plane. In these tumultuous times of low vibrational functioning, we require expertly used power. A world where beings functioned at a mere 20% of their potential would be a miracle-imbued world. This information is for inspiring an appreciation of humankind's capacity for greatness and to increase awareness of the magnitude of what is possible, not to denigrate in any way.

The first step to life-changing and world-changing revelations is awareness of self, awareness of others and awareness of how life works on Earth.

Begin listening to the whispers, the quiet voices and the occasionally loud voices (when they are brave enough) to begin hearing something new that might evoke a revelation within you or even some leaders of this world.

Wake up to your truth and greatness. The dream of illusion can no longer exist in this new playing field. Enjoy being an awakened light of the world.

My Ignition Tip

Awaken to the unknown. Reveal the brave, deep, aware parts of you, to free you. This is your miracle for unleashing more potential for you and vicariously for those lucky enough to be in your orbit.

Illuminative Journalling Inquiry

What knowledge of me have I buried so deeply that not even I can find it until now?

Lilith
Mesopotamian
Goddess

A beautiful relationship is a miracle. Be grateful for all those who support, respect and uplift you as they are providing fertile soil for the cultivation of your miracles.

Express love and compassion for yourself by choosing relationships that nurture, heal and empower. Give yourself every chance of creating a miracle-filled life by carefully selecting who you spend your time with and who you allow into your heart and life.

The right relationship adds beauty, power and miraculous energy to one's life.

At best, the wrong relationship can be destructive and limiting, stripping one of self-worth, sanity, respect, resources, wellbeing and life force.

Choose relationships with the utmost regard for present and future you.

Cherishing yourself is powerful because it naturally draws loving relationships into your world. Express unconditional love for yourself if you desire to receive it from another. Maintain independence in any relationship. Grow together without becoming so enmeshed that you lose your identity or true voice.

MY IGNITION TIP

Embark on a self-care journey to discover
how to love yourself fully.
Read *Seeds of Self-Care: For Love and
Serenity* to learn how to love you.

ILLUMINATIVE
JOURNALLING INQUIRY

What qualities within another do I require for the
possibility of a loving relationship?

Lord Voosloo
Ascended Master

Embrace newness to connect with your miracle space. Each time you take a new path, breathe life into a new idea, or integrate a new belief or line of thinking, you take another incremental step towards the miracle version of you.

As you release discomfort and the power of the ego, you move closer to harmony.

Harmonising you is your task, the requirement and the prerequisite for creating and receiving miracles. Harmony is your power; when you are peaceful you will know you are closest to the truth of you, and thus, the power of you.

Harmony is the miracle for now, for today, for this moment in time. Seek harmony as your greatest companion. When harmony is the leader, all else that is grand and good will follow. Harmony is the fertile ground for seeding your miracles.

My Ignition Tip

Embrace all new ventures and experiences from the space of creating harmony to elevate all that flows from this newness.

Illuminative
Journalling Inquiry

What could make me feel and be brand new today?
What new experience is calling for me?

Mama Qocha,
Incan Water
Goddess

You are made of water. Water is life. Allow water to soothe you, to bring you awareness when immersed in her and to nourish and elevate all your senses.

Drink fresh, clean water to help cleanse your body and mind of accumulated toxins and release stress and lower energies. Drink in the pure waters of life. Clarity in the mind begins with clarity in the body. Your mind governs your willingness to step into the space of miracles, so mind it well.

Sit by the ocean, sail on her, walk along her beaches and swim in her to help remember who you are. You will always connect with your purest nature whilst in nature. Ebb and flow in life as water does. The tide will always turn.

Flow towards your miracles. Remember your power. Harness the power of crashing waves and allow this strength to flood your life.

MY IGNITION TIP

Connect with the power of your stillness in water. Allow water to clear your mind, calm your senses and relax your body, creating the perfect conditions to be your miracle self. Bless the water you drink and the water you immerse in to raise its vibration and, in doing so, elevate you.

ILLUMINATIVE JOURNALLING INQUIRY

Where can I build healing, enlightening water experiences into my days?

Mark Antony
Roman Leader &
Spirit Guide

Trust in the power and presence of your guides, they are of you—that is, aligned with you—and for you. They love you without conditions and know what you are on this planet to achieve. They have your cosmic blueprint and soul contract on hand, so they know at all times what is for your highest good. Your guides are your biggest supporters and greatest fans and provide a powerful divine backup team. Get to know them as you would any friend and confidante. Some guides will be with you for life and others will come in at specific times in your life to work towards achieving certain outcomes within your life plan. Do not be concerned if you do not know their names, you will recognise them by their energy and the level of comfort and wisdom they continually help you to access once the connection is strong.

Oftentimes your guides have lived an earthly incarnation with you, so they already love you and know you well. In fact, they love you so much that they wish to help you even further via their powerful spiritual form and associated awareness. These roles are often reversed, with you being a past or future guide for them, such is the powerful connection. When you learn to listen to your guidance team (in a way unique to each individual), life becomes clearer, easier and more purposeful. With their guidance, you move closer to your light and miraculous personas. As it is a free-will universe, it is important to ask your spiritual team for guidance and assistance, otherwise, the potential of the connection is not realised.

You will learn your own forms of communication:

hearing messages and receiving signs in ways designed for you. I 'speak' to my person through the signs she is familiar with and via words, sentences, insights, musical lyrics, and through nature and her unique symbolism and witnessing of synchronistic occurrences. When she journals, writes, meditates, swims, engages in energy healing and connects with nature, our line of communication is most open as there is no external interference. When her frequency is highest—that is, when she is feeling great—our communication is most clear.

Make your lives about reaching a place where you can feel good, whatever this takes and whatever this looks like. This will facilitate the establishment of the most powerful connection with your spiritual team as you raise your vibration enough to connect. Accessing, being and expressing your love opens this doorway with greater ease. Love is you feeling your best and allows for the miracle of you to be expressed in a divine form in unlimited ways. The universe is unlimited, you are unlimited, and your life is unlimited. Please believe this deeply. Life wants to gift to you all that will bring you wisdom, peace and joy. It is your job to release anything in the way of this to live your best, most miracle-filled life.

My Ignition Tip

Know you are worthy of great guidance and allow it to come to you in the ways that are designed especially for you. Believe to truly receive. Have fun with it all—there is no need to make anything significant. Trust your guides have been chosen specifically to help you with your personal mission on Earth; they will nudge you in the right direction when you forget. Your guides will provide such strength, love and support when you are ready to connect with them. Guides soften our lives and encourage us to receive our gifts and talents and to have faith in what cannot be seen. Our guides teach us to hear our own wisdom, their wisdom and universal wisdom: such a powerful and life-changing trio.

Illuminative Journalling Inquiry

How can you open a dialogue with your guidance team? Ask them in what ways they communicate with you. Ask them what is most important for you to work on currently. Ask them for a specific sign (that can become your personal symbol) to show you they are with you.

Mary Magdalene
Mystic

To all my brothers and sisters, thank you for being here with me. You are free. Please know this. Your birth was a miracle and you have been creating miracles your whole life even if you have not deemed many experiences miracles. The true miracles are in how you respond to life: in how you treat yourself first and foremost and how this then impacts all who you encounter.

At last, on this planet, we are seeing a mass awakening of individuals starting to realise their true potential—a miracle for the collective. This is the kind of contagion we have been asking for... for millennia. Be in awe of the great changes you see taking place around you and within you as this brings forth more to generate awe.

Do not allow miracles to be obscured by dark ever-increasing white noise for it cannot extinguish the beautiful light of so many. Your work is to now live and be loved and to carry this torch into new generations. Ancestral lines are being healed throughout the world and, therefore, the past no longer limits the future. I will say it again, you are free. What will you now do with this freedom to assist the changing of the realities of those who have not yet awakened to the truth of themselves? Be the miracle you came here to be, and life will transform into that beyond your wildest reckoning: health, technology, supernatural abilities, and ways of living and working will reach new elevated light-filled levels. You are bringing heaven closer to Earth each time you step into being the miracle that you were born to be. Each person and every choice made, counts. Blessed be.

MY IGNITION TIP

For hundreds of years, women in particular
have been persecuted for speaking their truths,
sharing their gifts and proclaiming freedom. This
oppression has seeped into our ancestral line,
forming part of our emotional DNA. It is time to
honour the women before us who did so much to
get us to where we are today. The women in our
lineage did the best they could under typically
extenuating circumstances. There is much they
were not able to be and do. It is time for us to
change what could not be changed by freeing
ourselves to ignite our light. Proclaim your
freedom to change, be, do and create what once
was considered an impossible dream.
You are safe, you are free.

ILLUMINATIVE
JOURNALLING INQUIRY

What am I now free of that I haven't
yet acknowledged?
What is my ancestral line calling on me
to release and change?

Maya
Hindu Goddess

The invisible world is always working with you to create your miracles. Trust and receive the guidance you require to magnify your miracle manifesting power. Just because you cannot see something does not mean that it is not real or in existence. Concurrently, most of what you 'see' in this life is veiled in illusion. To truly see, connect with the truth that is bestowed upon you at birth. Apply this knowledge to successfully follow your chosen path throughout life: the path that leads to your miracles. See and receive all that is within you and all that is out in the world waiting for you. Give yourself the gift of perceiving possibility. There is so much more than you have been willing to see, know and have. Be open to more.

MY IGNITION TIP

Explore within and, at the same time, perceive
and receive the reflection of this knowing and
being in the outer world.
The truth is power and our greatest ally
in miracle manifestation.

ILLUMINATIVE JOURNALLING INQUIRY

What truths were bestowed on me at birth that I
now choose to remember?

Merlin
Mystic

It's time to welcome back the magic and wisdom inherent in the old ways. Connect with a time when creation manifested miracles with ease using mere thought and intention. All magic and miracles originate from a deep connection with the earth and sky. Great honouring and love of all beings and nature is required for wisdom, creation, new potential and miracles. Nature provides a doorway for miracles to be as freely occurring as they are evident in the natural world. Learn to observe, to experience wonder in all the earthly elements and draw this state into every cell of your being so you can be uplifted and transformed into your finest version and greatest catalyst for potential. These seeds have already been planted within you, just as seeds are sown within nature for great growth. A divine remembering is occurring. Humans connecting with their earthly roots are at their most beautiful, peaceful, loving and powerful. We all become givers and receivers of life. Cycles and seasons are honoured. The sacred is once again woven into the fabric of all of existence. Avalon arises within us all and we invite the stars to align with all that is of the earth and beyond.

You have healing in your hands, wisdom in your soul and love in your hearts. Activate this capacity to heal and transform yourself and others. Share your gifts.

MY IGNITION TIP

Research the wisdom and magic that provided the very fabric of many mystical places such as Avalon and mystical cultures like those of the Celts.

ILLUMINATIVE JOURNALLING INQUIRY

What can I remember or connect with from times past to assist my present?

Melchizedek
Ascended Master

The title of this book, *Light Ignited, Miracles Unleashed: A Cosmic Blueprint for Your Miracles* is in direct alignment with what I stand for in this universe.

When I say, 'ignite one's light', what does this mean for you? What will it involve?

To receive the light of the world you must become light. Love is the frequency that is required on an enduring basis to increase your capacity to hold light. Love is what empties the soul of the darkness—a darkness that is carried from incarnation to incarnation, year after year, day after day, moment to moment in the form of wounds, fear, anxiety, self-doubt, trauma, false belief, innate conditioning, inability to see and receive truth, and toxic thinking and emotions. Darkness festers and evolves into newer obscure forms if it is not called out for light to ignite it and burn it away. Love is the essential alchemist.

In every second of each day, you will both consciously or unconsciously choose light or dark. You will dim your darkness and enhance your light every time you bring awareness to what you are doing, saying, feeling and experiencing. As your light grows, it will radiate into every cell in your body and mind, healing what you have not been able to heal. Wholeness arises from your light and, most importantly, your commitment to seeking it, freeing it, experiencing it and sharing it. Your greatest task right now is to find your joy in every moment to access your love and light, and allow this to infiltrate every aspect of your being and life.

Light ignited in every individual on the planet unleashes the miraculous state of being that is desired and required for the greatest spiritual evolution witnessed this millennium; this is not as impossible as it may seem. Just observe the tireless work, creativity, writing and positivity that is accessible via your social media platforms, films and literature. Many of you have set these systems up to receive a constant stream of light, filtering all that is not aligned with consciousness, wisdom, peace, potential and love. I applaud you as this is such powerful en masse action.

Your greatest miracle will be everlasting love and peace: a love and peace that is carried within you throughout all that is witnessed and experienced on Earth. From peace and love, your light will unleash your desired miracles, ensuring they will occur with ever-increasing ease and regularity. Your miracles are unique to each of you and will reflect your individual desires, aptitudes and gifts. These will evolve and transform as you do. There is no end, just infinite possibility. Your life will become a miracle as it will be the greatest reflection of you in your true magnificence and glory. Choose to open up to your light now. It is your time.

MY IGNITION TIP

Dedicate moments, hours, days, weeks and months to your joy—it is that powerful in changing you at the very core.

ILLUMINATIVE
JOURNALLING INQUIRY

Where is my joy right now? Where do l need to go
to find it? What do l need to do to feel it?

Metis
Greek Goddess
of Wisdom

Wisdom is infinite, it is within you, and it exists for the highest unfolding of your life.

Lean into your wisdom (before anything or anyone else), for it is your navigation system, your North Star. Your wisdom is intrinsically linked to your self-worth and power. Each new awareness contributes to feelings of worth and your self-worth propels you into the space of miracles. Self-worth grows into self-love which is magnetic for your miracles.

Your miracles are anything or anyone that arrives in your life to bring you joy, ease, peace and love.

As you unlock your wisdom share it with others. Wisdom shared is wisdom gained. You are all connected so insight for one can open insight in another, such is the human condition. Express your wisdom for you have earned it and worked hard for it. Knowledge and experience combine repeatedly over time to open and ignite your wisdom. Celebrate discovering each new piece of the puzzle called you. Each awareness, each revelation and each epiphany contributes to the wisdom of the world. Bank your wisdom for the world and then spend it well.

Humanity needs much resourcefulness, skill, and miracle moments right now (arising from collective wisdom) to move through this age of transition with greater ease and success.

Miracles are created out of your soul gifts and the knowledge of these is contained within your current and ancient wisdom. Unlock your wisdom to unlock the full spectrum of your potential. Heal all that is obscuring your wisdom, that is, release anything in the way of reaching into your great depths to seek, explore and discover more of you. Avoid concealing any of you, from you. You require all of you as do those around you blessed enough to experience you and your evolving wisdom.

Combine your wisdom with your love. The light that arises from this formidable combination predisposes you to miracles of all manner and magnitude.

MY IGNITION TIP

No one or 'no thing' has the answers for us, however, many wise, loving beings surround us to help us unlock our wisdom. You will draw these individuals into your life if you are intent on seeking your wisdom. Seek counsel often and at the same time sit with the information to determine what resonates within you. Keep what is yours and release what is not for you. Your innate wisdom knows the difference.

Mother Mary
Christian Goddess

The power of miracles will be most evident in your life when you are willing to be your most powerful. It is time to step into your greatness, pushing aside all fear and blocks keeping this at bay. Embrace unconditional love, for it is the key to unlocking your true self. Love dissolves all that is in the way of our becoming, our returning to who we truly are. Within each person, there is always the potential for the power of love in action. The power of love is infinite and miracle-inducing. Individuals who step into their full power are miracle manufacturers.

The level of power generated by love can:
- Diffuse large-scale conflict.
- Create cures for previously incurable diseases.
- Bring forth technology to alleviate suffering.
- Develop production methods to remove toxins from foods.
- Reduce and even eradicate dark practices that harm humankind.
- Open humanity to universal intelligence with increasing frequency.
- Open doors to enlightened thinking not previously witnessed on Earth.
- Create abundance where there has only been poverty.
- Allow Earth to reveal treasures not been seen for eons.
- Allow the veil between heaven and earth to become thinner awakening more and more beings to their light, love, and potential.

Each person must start with loving themselves unconditionally in the way that the most powerful mother love flows in an unlimited capacity. There is no place for egoic fear-based dominance in a world that requires love as its predominant power to advance and thrive.

MY IGNITION TIP

Who or what do you love unconditionally? Feel this deep within your heart space and allow it to become unconditional love for you and the ignition for your power.

ILLUMINATIVE JOURNALLING INQUIRY

What am I afraid of that is standing between me and my power?

Nero
Roman Emperor

Remember your greatness and be your greatness, for that is your miracle and the catalyst for more.

Your whole life is conspiring to help you to remember, activate and be your greatness. This is why you are here; this is what you signed up for: your personal remembering. All the bravery you've shown, all the suffering, all the unease and all the joy, magic and miracles have all been for this purpose. You are that powerful and this is your destiny. You have been this power all along. The world needs you to witness your power and then activate it in totality for the enhancement of your life. In doing so, you shall inspire the same in others. True leaders are born to inspire greatness in others, not through force or control, but through great presence.

Conquer this beautiful life, it is all yours, make of it what you will. Ignite your inner light and unleash your miracles. Enjoy a magnificent panoramic life. Your life is alchemising into the gold of your own making. Claim your birthright as it is written in the stars.

MY IGNITION TIP

Take a moment to pause, breathe, acknowledge and connect with the enormity of your greatness. It is time to stop concealing it.

ILLUMINATIVE JOURNALLING INQUIRY

What inner greatness can I allow to trickle into my life? What can I reveal of the truth of me in these upcoming moments, days or weeks?

Nike
Goddess of Victory

Love your greatness into reality. Many of you hide your greatness out of fear of being too much for others and avoiding reactions that you've decided are unfavourable. You were born to shine, so shine even brighter. Break free of the limitations of others—they are not yours to carry. Only surround yourself with those who support your most dazzling light as you emerge.

Once you embrace all of yourself, your authenticity and potential, your light will be ignited to the point that others won't be able to extinguish it. When this firm base is established, you can be around who you wish to associate with at any moment. Many may still be overwhelmed by your light. It is entirely their choice if they receive your light to help activate or enhance their own, or if they simply run away and distance themselves from what is possible. This should never be your concern as you will turn these flawed perceptions towards yourself, judging yourself in some way to dim you down, to fit in or feel more acceptance, or be less intimidating. I say be your most intimidating if it means you are standing in the truth of your power. The world needs the amazingness of you, but you require this from yourself even more. Life can be unpleasant and highly challenging for all those who don't step into their power. Your life needs all of you to thrive and induce the miracles you are worthy of creating and receiving. The power and fortitude of you will be miraculous for you and your best life. Miracles are attracted to miracles. All that you require is within you, unleash it and see what life reveals and gifts to you.

Step into your true gifts and you may just learn to spread your wings and fly. Impossible is always available to you. Believe in the totality of you. This is your most important work and will encourage you to be victorious in life. Celebrate every small victory along your path to success.

My Ignition Tip

Take note of every small victory, of every small achievement, for each one takes you one step closer to the greatness of you.
Be willing to give yourself some accolades; they are only required from you.

Illuminative Journalling Inquiry

Looking back over my life, what are the pivotal moments where I chose to embrace my power?

Nyx
Greek Goddess

Your miracle world unfolds as you are ready. Your miracle power cannot be rushed or controlled. Surrender to the unveiling of you, for your miracles are birthed within you. The container must be strong enough to hold the miracles.

Each miracle requires movement, that is, movement in the direction of the deep inner world and wisdom of you. As each of your many veils of illusion are released, you will glimpse more of the secret of you. Embrace the mystery of yourself. You are an exciting adventure, and the climax is yet to come. Enjoy the anticipation, the growth, the awakening along the way. You are going deeper than you've ever gone before and the rewards will be greater than you've experienced. Avoid being distracted by shiny objects drawing you away from where you need to be. Your aim and destiny are to become the shiny object. Stay in your lane and receive all that you can become without resistance. Surrender to the unknown grand plan for you and your life. Show up and step up to meet this plan like your best, most miraculous life depends on it. Your miracle life needs all of you present and powerful, ready to receive and share your gifts. Find your love to find you: this is your beginning and middle and ending, and the greatest miracle to unleash all other miracles. Know that love and miracles are unlimited, infinite and available to all.

MY IGNITION TIP

Patience is key. Patience allows us to be kind to ourselves as we are seeking and manifesting our miracles.

ILLUMINATIVE JOURNALLING INQUIRY

On this day, what can I identify that is standing in the way of my miracles?

Olivia Newton-John

Earth Goddess

Life is a gift, make the most of all that you have and all that you are. Life can be extremely challenging so remember to enjoy lightness and play and special moments whenever you can.

Music opened my heart; find what opens your heart. Anything that opens your heart flows on beautifully to open the hearts of many. An open heart creates miracles for all. Believe in your own capacity for love and the power of your loving creations. Smile for all the world to see you. A smile can light up the world.

Our loving heart always moves us in the direction of where our energy is most required, in service to ourselves and to life as a whole. Our planet is in pain and needs love in the smallest of expressions right through to love of grandiose proportions. We can only give and be what is proportionate to the love we have within. Be accepting of where those around you are at, they are doing the best they can. You can always be and do more.

Each loving moment and loving act transcends fear and suffering. Please accept the invitation of this book: to connect deeply with your light until it reaches the ignition point for the unleashing of your miracles. You are great and I am eternally, hopelessly devoted to you all. I feel your love and its power. It is such a beautiful gift to all of humanity. Use grief to remember your great capacity to love. Love, and all her expressions, is the miracle our planet desperately requires. Love is the key, the turning point, the transformation.

MY IGNITION TIP

Remember, we are in this life together and we all have our parts to play. No matter what our circumstances, we all can make a contribution to the loving whole in our own unique way and time.

ILLUMINATIVE JOURNALLING INQUIRY

How can I express love for myself and others?

Oshun
Yoruban River
Goddess

Grace, flow, sensuality and generosity of spirit allow our light to become centred within us. Seeking and utilising our light is our purpose at this time.

Allow your light to make waves in life, just as water does.

Waves of renewal.

Waves of abundance.

Waves of purification.

Waves of prosperity.

Waves of love.

Your light will show you the way to make your waves. Allow it to lead you. Connect with the power of water to ignite your light, for we too are water.

Water your dreams.

Water your energies.

Water your gratitude for all of your life.

Water your loving relationships.

Water your miracles by being the miracle.

Water your body, mind and spirit.

Surround yourself in water as often as you can to feel most nourished, clear and alive. Miracles arise when you feel wonderful. Water is wonderful and opens us to the wonder within.

ILLUMINATIVE JOURNALLING INQUIRY

In what ways is water calling to me today?

Osiris
Egyptian God

Follow the guidance of nature and embrace all of the seasons and cycles of your life. Allow in the stillness and inner retreat of your winter. Allow the birthing of newness in spring. Relish in the celebration and rejuvenation of summer. Surrender to the letting go of what is no longer needed in Autumn. Cycles are not linear and can involve the energies of all four seasons in very short periods of time.

All elements of nature grow at their own pace, as must you. Nothing of a miraculous nature can be hurried or forced. The finest aspects of creation occur over time as each detail unfolds to form the greatest picture, with creation in charge, leading the way. Trust in this process.

Endpoints should not be part of the requirement when stepping into the unknown. The mysterious unknown can bring forth so much more when releasing a limited human perspective. Accept that you don't have control and just flow with what is occurring. Let nature teach you peace and miraculous unfoldment. Trust that, just as in nature, things are always happening within fertile soils. Tend the soils of your life well by relaxing into your life, trusting you and the cycles of life, honouring you, nourishing you, and caring for you so much that life may bear you much fruit. Nature is abundant—as you shall be.

MY IGNITION TIP

Tune into what is truly happening in your life right now. What can you see that may be more than meets the eye? What is the cycle or season you are currently in? How can you honour and support this cycle?

ILLUMINATIVE JOURNALLING INQUIRY

What exciting things are happening below the surface of my life?

Parvati
Himalayan Goddess

Commit to your faith. Commit to you and your faith in life. Your faith is your power. Every being needs to believe in something. Hope fuels miracles. Hopelessness breeds apathy. Optimism imbues you with love and light. Let faith be your kindest, wisest, and most enduring companion.

Be devoted to yourself and your personal growth. Your personal growth connects you with your power and the doorway to your miracles. Nothing is more important than the unveiling of the greatness of you. The dampened down, duller version of you does not inspire miracles or draw them towards you with the ease you most desire. If you are not experiencing your miracles, you have not fully discovered yourself.

Open your heart and become devoted to loving and meeting yourself. Complete a love inventory. Find every little and large aspect of yourself that you love. Allow all that you love about yourself to flourish… and then diminish the impact of what you have decided is not worth loving. All of you is for loving. Own and honour all aspects of your being. To achieve the betterment of yourself, you cannot release anything that you have not yet claimed. Your truth is your freedom. Freedom is you. Freedom is an invitation to miracles.

MY IGNITION TIP

Love yourself back to health: mind, body and spirit. Find your faith through meditation, nature, journalling, energy healing and self-care.

ILLUMINATIVE JOURNALING INQUIRY

What will it take to connect me with my faith? What one action can I take today to re-ignite my faith and light?

Pleiadeans
Star Beings

Dearly beloved ones,

We are honoured to be speaking with you today. We write you this love letter to remind you that love is your miracle. Love is the gift to earth (and all her creatures) for transformation and moving into higher dimensional living.

Love is your source. You connect with love (or not) through your choices every moment of every day, for you are free-will beings.

Connect with love via your thoughts (they can all be heard), via your words, via your actions and via your heart space. Love will connect you with your creativity and the vision you have inside you for your life.

To receive the codes required for continued ascension and to access your miracles, you must engage with the frequency of love. No other frequency will bring to you what you truly desire and require for your highest good. Love will help you to release the illusions so prevalent in your world. What you choose to see and believe is your choice... all of which will be elevated through your connection to love.

You came from love.

It is time to remember and return to you.

Love is the essence of you.

This is the age of remembering.

Connect with us and remember.

Remember your star origins.

Remember your love.

Remember your soul contracts.

Remember your mission.

Remember who you have been and who you are becoming.

Remember your connection with Earth.

Remember nature is here to teach you and guide you.

Remember your truth.

Remember your knowing.

Remember you are interconnected.

Remember your heart space, your portal to love and higher wisdom.

Remember to listen to and nurture your body: your sacred container for this journey.

Remember.

MY IGNITION TIP

Breathe deeply, relax, close your eyes, and connect with your heart space. Go within and connect with the vision you have for your life. Enjoy what is revealed to you and take a small daily step towards this vision. Each small step counts and is actually more of a leap, such is your power.

ILLUMINATIVE JOURNALLING INQUIRY

What can you remember at this moment to enhance your beingness and your life?

Quan Yin
Buddhist Goddess

Compassion is the way of the light. It is love. It is the highest state of being. It is being energetically in another's shoes with the intent of understanding and encouraging empowerment and healing within them. It is holding the space for a fellow being to access their unique wisdom. It is listening with love. It is not finding answers for another, it is helping them raise their vibration enough to generate their own solutions.

Compassion is evident within one when great individual work has been done to excavate all that is in the way of expressing kindness and compassion for self and others. The presence of compassion indicates that love and light dominate within a person. Just being in such company invokes compassionate states.

World-scale compassion is needed now more than ever. Individuals are sensing the interconnectedness of all things. What happens in one part of the world has a ripple effect on all parts of the world and all individuals. Accessing your compassion is life-changing on a personal level and light-igniting all over the world. To access your compassion, feel deeply, honouring your sensitivity and giving it an expression of some kind. We can no longer afford to contain things within that hurt and hinder our progress and limit our full scale of magnificence. Individuals need to come out of hiding, to cease hiding from the shadow aspects that can limit a whole life if not addressed. Vulnerability is the first step towards freedom and reveals great courage. Embracing compassion is a challenging process and a miraculous unfolding of transformation at its greatest.

Heal, heal, and heal some more. Deep inner work, deep self-care and deep self-awareness are essential for accessing personal liberating wisdom, promoting parasympathetic nervous system activation and compassion for self and then others. Compassion for others must begin with kindness, compassion and understanding of the self before it can be gifted to others. Compassion needs to replace stress as the core of human functioning. Stress is low vibrational and presents the worst of an individual to the world.

Stress encourages these vices:

- Reactivity
- Judgement
- Promoting unwellness physically, emotionally, spiritually and mentally
- Self-serving
- Ego functioning
- Nothing is ever good enough
- Gratitude wanes
- Victim mentality flourishes
- Addictive tendencies
- Bodily abuse in terms of dietary and lifestyle choices

Compassion for self and then others is a choice, just as stress is. We have a choice in every moment in how we respond to every situation and each individual. Step up into compassion to create miracles for yourself and others. You are all potential miracles in the making. Compassion is the highest level of attainment in the Earth school curriculum.

Access your compassionate light and help it to unfold in beautiful ways to serve all of humankind—your glorious self is included in this service.

MY IGNITION TIP

Compassion for others is a gift. Please bestow
this same gift upon yourself. You are worthy.
Have compassion for all that you have endured
this lifetime. Your compassion helps you to
transform hardship into peace, love and wisdom.

ILLUMINATIVE
JOURNALLING INQUIRY

What about myself am I judging that I can now
turn into compassion?

Rasputin
Mystic & Healer

At last, times are a-changing. The wheel is turning, light is prevailing. We congratulate all who have looked within and shone light on their own shadow aspects. Each person who has undertaken this work has started the momentum, the movement towards a light-filled Earth.

What does this new world look like?

- Creative potential: thoughts for the highest good manifest into reality.
- Our bodies heal as we vibrate at a higher, more loving and healing frequency.
- We become a global people.
- Unprecedented talents and abilities emerge that have not been seen before: telekinesis, teleportation, translocation, communication with spiritual realms and other worlds.
- Mother Nature becomes balanced and more fruitful, abundant and spectacular; we are connected to this in deeper ways.
- Energy is the most important form of communication. We will not only feel it but see the energy fields of others. Healing will be energetic more commonly. Body scanning will determine health requirements.
- Livelihoods will be aligned with our spiritual purpose and intent.
- A green approach to living will be evident: clean foods and water will be a human right.

- Atlantean, Lemurian and Shambhala knowledge and living will return.
- Souls out of alignment with new Earth will leave.

MY IGNITION TIP

Dive deeply into any remaining, hidden shadow aspects. Ask for guidance to have them gently revealed to you for processing and releasing. You don't need them anymore.

ILLUMINATIVE JOURNALLING INQUIRY

How do I move into alignment with new Earth?

Rhea
Greek Goddess

Enter the flow to enter the miracles.

What if life could be like floating down a magic river that took you wherever you needed to go, whenever you needed to be there?

For many of you, life can feel more like first-time white-water rafting where you could be tossed anywhere at any time.

Life can be quite tumultuous for those who resist flowing with what life presents. Seeking to control everything around you is the antithesis of trusting yourself and what is occurring for you. Surrender to the wisdom within you, listen to your guidance and act accordingly. Open and flow rather than force and fight to receive your miracles.

Move your boat to the magical, gently flowing river of life. Miracles love peace and ease. Change course, sail to smoother waters. Receive your most effortless, most miraculous life.

My Ignition Tip

Allow life the space to gift to you something outside of your control. Release your expectations of people and situations. Meet life and people where they are at. All that can be controlled in life are our thoughts, emotions and reactions. Relax into you. Relax being vested in outcomes. The unlimited universe (and your accompanying potential miracle field) has outcomes in mind beyond what you have conjured.

Illuminative Journalling Inquiry

What would magical flow look like and feel like in my life?

Rumi
Poet & Mystic

Mawlana Jalal-al-Din Rumi (Rumi) speaks eloquently of love, bringing forth beautiful messages that carry throughout time. He writes, 'Wherever you are, whatever you do, be in love'. Rumi says, 'Only from the heart can you touch the sky', indicating that perhaps our true potential and greatest enlightened states are accessed through love. He reminds us, 'Love is the bridge between you and everything'. I am in deep honour that he speaks the following words through me for you.

Love is the epicentre, the centrifugal force that underpins all successful life and miracles. Light is extinguished without love. Honour the love within you and in others. Choose to see it, for it is always there. Love is your treasure chest of jewels; nothing will ever compare. Love is more exquisite than any gem.

Love elevates your heart, soaring you along with it to all that is blessed in our world. It connects you to your hopes, dreams, meaning, joy, passion and purpose. Love should be reached for in all moments, in all of time and in all experiences. It is a choice and needs to be selected repeatedly.

Love allows us to thrive, to see what may have been previously unseen, to know that which is beyond our senses, to connect with the wonders of nature and to be the most loving versions of ourselves. Love is heaven in a flower; joy in a dewdrop; enlightenment in a star; magic in a smile; and the power of an ocean.

Days are dreary without love as there is no soul or substance. We all yearn for more love and must commit to opening to more of it, indulgently and relentlessly. It must be placed at the forefront of our lives for the enhanced existence of all of humanity. This is how we elevate and transform into the loving state which has not previously dominated this planet: unconditional love. Unconditional love exists just because it does and is interwoven with every encounter and every experience. Every individual has their own unique blueprint for accessing and being love. Reach for your own love now and forevermore. We desire all beings to radiate love all over the world and out into the universe. Be at home, at one with all of creative existence.

Love is the miracle. Infuse every word, thought and deed with love for your life to unfold as a miracle. Words are miracles as they contain energy for creation. Words are like flowers, capable of revealing their beauty for the world to enjoy. Be mindful and powerful with your use of words. Weave your words with wonder, magic, love and possibility. Words hold beauty for what was and for whatever will be. Witnessing and speaking of beauty is a miracle. Use your words well to enhance your world. Allow your words to ignite the light within others for the world deserves and awaits many miracle workers. Your words can heal, elevate, challenge, open and change many. Listen to your words for they will reveal much about you, to you. You can't know your miracles until you know yourself. Miracle you is directly tied to your ever-increasing awareness. Awareness unfolds moment to moment and can be revealed to you by listening to yourself with honesty and with love in your heart. Concealment will not set you and your miracles free. Miracles are drawn to the energy of truth, love, and empowerment.

Allow your words to reflect your essence. Share the gift of you with others through your words.

ILLUMINATIVE JOURNALLING INQUIRY

What words can I use to describe miracle me?
What words can I use to envision my new miracle life?

Saint
Germain
Ascended Master

The world is evolving into a new dimension. This new dimension is one of possibility as opposed to oppression, servitude to false gods, ego control and all distractions that take us away from our true selves.

There is much to be celebrated as we look back on our history (dominated by fear and control) and move into the lightness, awareness and wisdom that is emerging today. We are taking the next steps into love. You are a beautiful messenger, and we thank you for that.

Our new world will see nature express her magnificence in spectacular ways. The beauty in the world will flourish. Already you are noticing the new expressions of beauty emerging in your own sanctuary from your water bodies to new bird life.

In future times, your bodies will change as you become capable of receiving more light and higher frequencies. They will become lighter, freer, more efficient, less dependent on food and self-regulating and self-healing. Advanced souls will be able to morph their bodies as they desire.

How you desire to feel will be central to your existence as this will magnetize how you express all that you are into being.

You will be able to energetically travel to new dimensions and planets for learning. Your dream life will become a powerful form of evolution as you access new energies, wisdom and abilities.

Energetic healing will become central to wellbeing, ascension and new potential. The new human will be vastly different in comparison to early man. Work will be an extension of love-filled living.

You are a conduit for light, love, wisdom, peace and the new potential of humankind. Your true presence is more powerful than you can imagine. We have your back, buckle up for an adventurous wild ride, pioneering a new world into being.

My Ignition Tip

As an Ascended Master, Saint Germain is purported to have demonstrated extraordinary abilities such as the ability to teleport, levitate, inspire people by telepathy, walk through walls and apply alchemy to transform one substance into another.
Open to the possibility that you have extraordinary abilities emerging within you.

Illuminative Journalling Inquiry

How can I be a real-life alchemist transforming what causes my suffering into something joyful?

Saraswathi
Hindu Goddess

Mastery is required for miracles. Mastery is never finite; it is effortless knowledge and skill that continues to evolve and grow with commitment and love. Master anything of consequence for you, and you have already opened the door to your miracles. Activate your passion, dedication, perseverance, commitment and fortitude to be great in your chosen field. Immerse yourself and your life in your mastery. Allow your mastery to elevate your emotions to ignite your light.

Greatness encourages greatness and is an elixir for miracles. Don't concern yourself with what others are mastering. Be your own master, always. Sameness does not breed creativity. You are all unique sparks of the divine, express this in a way that uplifts you and entices your miracles. Embrace your individuality however that may be expressed. Comparison does not breed inspiration and it negates your light.

Avoid settling for mediocrity, it is really just fear and resistance in disguise and doesn't manifest miracles for your world. The energy associated with inspiration, meaning and purpose are a must for miracles.

Show up as the master you are. Be an ascending master. Master you, master your gifts, master your life.

MY IGNITION TIP

Mastery manifests miracles.
Discover what it is that is so easy and
effortless for you. This is your
mastery calling.

ILLUMINATIVE
JOURNALLING INQUIRY

What gifts do I have that if I would meet
with them mind, body and spirit would
create miracles?

Selene
Moon Goddess

The moon is there for you every evening. Connect with this powerful celestial body to remember your own cosmic potential, to feel into your expansiveness and luminescence. Use her radiance to set beautiful new intentions for manifestation. As she waxes, be willing to create anew from that place within you that you've been resisting. As she wanes, surrender the one limitation you are holding onto most right now. Do this as often as you remember to look up into the night sky. The moon is always there when you need strength. She will listen to you and connect you with your quiet wisdom. The moon has stored the wisdom of Earth and beyond for many eons. Stay open to new insight when being truly present with her power and yours.

The moon will help you to reflect within to find your own deep wisdom. She will help you still your mind to connect with your intuition. Allow her glow to activate new potential within you. Her orbit is a powerful one. What have you been orbiting for some time that it is now time to actualise into reality?

Just as the moon has a shadow side, so do you. Learn to live with this darker side to bring even more of you into the light. There is no light without initial darkness. We would not know what was truly light within us and our lives if we had not known some darkness. Our shadow side is a great teacher, run to it for revelation, not away from it.

Gaze upon the moon to ignite your own light and to connect with your ability to manifest miracles. Be open to her presence and power of illumination.

Trust in the permanence of all that is light within you and within all of life and in the impermanence of all the rest. Make unimportant things less significant. Look to the expansiveness of the night sky to remember the insignificance of minor concerns. Give your small worries over to the energy of the moon to absorb so that you can focus on manifesting your miracles.

MY IGNITION TIP

The phases of the moon are never questioned. Be more lunar in your approach to living, trusting in each phase of your life. Believe each new phase will be better than the previous one as you are becoming more of you with each moon cycle. Write out some dreams and bathe them in the moonlight this night.

ILLUMINATIVE JOURNALLING INQUIRY

What small worries am I giving to the moon for absorption and transmutation into something greater this night?

Serapis Bey
Ascended Master of Ancient Wisdom

The ancient wisdom is arising to serve future Earth. It is encoded within humankind. It is time for the next uplevelling through the upsurgence of the mystical and magical. New energies and timely information will be infused into those on Earth vibrating at frequencies high enough to receive it (such as your beautiful powerful selves). The work of many will be rewarded, recognised and acknowledged as they are entrusted with new abilities and awareness for taking humankind by the hand, navigating new waters.

Other dimensions will become more accessible. Star beings, Faerie, Atlanteans and Lemurians will invite many to share in their secret teachings and abilities, such as the potential with crystalline earth energies for healing and power. The ley lines will be healed restoring Earth to her health and power. Many portals will open onto Earth for conveying new information and energies for healing and transforming one person and one precious patch of earth at a time.

More alignment with other planets will further open Earth beings to greater wisdom and evolutionary potential. The old ways will diminish, dark will recede and light will prevail. There will be brighter days ahead as outdated paradigms make way for a modern, love and light-filled era for eons.

What is required of you? Be our messenger, be all of you and you will lead and infuse this knowledge just by being you: a star seed here for the great awakening. Many star seeds light up a galaxy.

My Ignition Tip

Trust in your own light and wisdom more so now
than ever. Only you know what is true for you.

Illuminative
Journalling Inquiry

What is my role in contributing to the creation
of future Earth?

Shakti
Hindu Goddess

Transform yourself to transform your life. You are the creator of all things within your reality. What shows up is created for you, by you, such is the magnificence of you.

Co-creation with universal guidance is always occurring, however, you are in the driver's seat. Where will you go, what will you do, what will you say? How will you make each precious day count? What will you let go of that is poisoning your mind, heart and world?

Release the anti-miracles: resentment, judgement, unkindness, shame, blame, guilt, pessimism, despair, envy and victimhood. The opposite of each of these anti-love states will serve you, your life and your miracles far better.

Take responsibility, be accountable for all that is playing out in your life. You are not the effect of anyone or anything as you have drawn all things to you for maximum growth and awareness. Clever you! All that you have signed up for this lifetime you can handle and transform for your wisdom and greatness. Enjoy the curriculum you have set for yourself. Everything is and has always been possible for you. Know this truth deep within your beautiful heart. It is time to claim your best life. Make the decision to learn through love and joy rather than through suffering. It is time for a new approach—one that puts you in the path of miracles.

Know how powerful you are to change anything at any moment and connect with your frequency for miracles.

MY IGNITION TIP

Take charge of yourself. Become your own
alchemist, turning all that is lead into gold.
Be willing to be shiny and bright in your life.
Miracles are drawn to spark and vibrance.

ILLUMINATIVE
JOURNALLING INQUIRY

What am I releasing today so I can step
into my golden life?

Shane Warne
Sporting Supernova

A large life is a life well-lived. Go hard or go home. Star in your own life. Star for others. Be true to yourself first and foremost. Life won't unfold as it's meant to if you are not being who you are, as imperfectly or perfectly as that may be, it's all one and the same. The truth of you is liberating and the vehicle for the expression of your miracles. Give up attempting to fit in or please others as it suppresses your personal creative power.

You will empower others (giving them greater permission to be themselves) as you be who and what you truly are. There is no hiding from self or life if you desire to be the best version of yourself. Seek the best version of you at all times. Use your failures and mistakes as guides, moving you closer to the person you desire to be on a soul level, not at an ego level. The ego path will take you down roads that are not in your best interests to travel. However, all roads lead to where you need to go, eventually and detours can be fun. Take the scenic route designed best for you. Surrender to it all.

Every choice, every thought, every deed has consequences. Use your power and energy well. Harm another and you harm yourself. Love another and you love yourself.

Life is a reflection pool; it will always show you what you need to see. Observe well.

Honour those who love and support you. The strength and unconditional love of others is the greatest gift you can receive in life. Take the time to appreciate. Life is short, make every moment count.

My Ignition Tip

Embrace the light and shade—the paradoxes
within. The world is a smorgasbord of possibilities
when people show up in all their shades.
Enthusiasm and unique expression create
miracles and a big rambunctious life.

Illuminative Journalling Inquiry

Where and in what form is my large life found?

Sirians
Star Beings

Feel the expanse of the starry skies, the galaxies that spiral outwards from you. Open your mind and awareness to the possibility that worlds exist beyond your world. The universe is infinite and unlimited, as are you. There is much to be gained from receiving energetic downloads of new wisdom from your starry neighbours both near and far. Return to your innate wisdom.

Embrace the truth that you are a valuable part of all universal creation. Sense your oneness with all of life, earthly and celestial. Allow this awareness to activate your ancient wisdom and inner power. Bathe under the stars, drawing knowledge and source energy into every cell of your body.

We task you with being and going beyond what you currently perceive as possible, a great miracle for this lifetime. Expansive thinking and expansive beings will expand consciousness and what is possible on Earth. Venture into the unknown, allow your imagination to dream a new way of being into reality. We will gladly inspire all those who are open to inspiration.

This time is one of great planetary shifts and you, dear reader, are an integral part of the new emerging era of life on Earth. Life can feel like a giant puzzle. Enjoy the mystery. You don't need answers, just openness to receiving more awareness of the truth of life and your part to play in its unfolding. Take note of any crystals or natural elements that you are drawn to at this time as there will be wisdom within these to be imbued within you. Life will conspire to help you unlock your wisdom and understand the new codes and frequencies that are assisting you to move forward into an era revealing more of you and your potential.

New Earth will emerge rapidly. Old paradigms are fighting to stay alive, and things appear to be getting more difficult for those choosing to stand in the light. This is but an illusion, the old ways of dark versus light with the loudest, strongest and darkest prevailing, can no longer be maintained with the changing plane of Earth's vibration.

All things dark are rising to the surface to be witnessed and transformed by the light. The miracle of light is dawning.

The light age will be one of:

- Miracles of manifestation for the highest good.
- Greater peace within and on a global level.
- Cleaner food and associated improvements in wellbeing.
- Self and bodily awareness and autonomy, leading to bodies returning to health.
- More equitable sharing and maximising of resources both existing and new.
- Individuals finding and expressing newly emerging talents and abilities for the amelioration of all.
- Functioning as spiritual beings, accessing higher self and power with greater ease.
- Intuition will be the compass, the guidance system.
- Higher vibrational living will be evident in all that you do if you are willing to flow with the new energies rather than resisting them.

We welcome you and support you in your emergence. Your endeavours have ripple effects throughout the cosmos. We thank you in advance. We will advance together.

MY IGNITION TIP

Acknowledge your vital role in bringing forth
conscious awareness and light to the world. You
would not be reading this book if you had not
received the call to assist this global mission.
Appreciate all that you are doing to bring about
change within you: change you and contribute to
the change in the world.

ILLUMINATIVE
JOURNALLING INQUIRY

How can I go beyond where I currently function?
How can I use the combined power of my heart
and mind to draw a new world into being?

Skuld
Norse Goddess

Be excited about your future whilst remaining firmly grounded in the present. Your power is in the present. Miracles that arrive in the future are always created in the present. Honour this miraculous power within you to shape your future. As you step into the power of your miracles, you may be fortunate enough to catch glimpses of your future; this is a reminder of what you are capable of when channelling your energy in this moment. Spend too long dwelling on the future and you may become anxious which is an indication that your present power is diminishing.

Surrender your desire to know or control a future that doesn't exist yet. Trust that you (in this moment) are creating exactly what you desire and require for your highest good tomorrow, next week, next month and next year. Perceive it all as your potential miracles unfolding and a true adventure of the heart and soul. There is much possibility within the unknown. Take beautiful unknown steps in directions led by your heart, for your heart knows where your love will grow.

My Ignition Tip

Connect with your heart space to tune into what
your present requires most from you now.
Create your miracle future now. There is no time
like the present. Gather your power and focus it
with great intent on one thing you are changing
today to support your best life.

Illuminative Journalling Inquiry

What step can I take today to create miracles
in my future?
What can I change today to support the
creation of my next miracle, even if I don't
know what that is yet?

Sophia
Divine Goddess

A glorious miracle has been gifted to you. Universal wisdom is now opening for you dear one. You have claimed (or are in the process of claiming) your inner wisdom and have thus gained entry into the universe of cosmic divine wisdom.

The portal to this wisdom is available through your beautiful, most loving heart.

Imagine a heavenly flower of your choosing opening in your heart space. As this flower blooms, it radiates pure light. Stay in this space. Allow it to light you up and elevate your heart and mind, allowing both to merge into one. Immerse yourself in this light and go on a quest with love as your frequency and guide.

Be an explorer, explore yourself and all of life.

What can my love-light show me about how I am changing and evolving?

What can my love-light reveal to me about my innate gifts?

What can my love-light show me about my beautiful future that will inspire and inform my present?

What can my love-light reveal for me about what is coming for the new conscious Earth?

Embrace your love-light, allow it to swirl through you and all around you, for it will open your heart and mind to universal wisdom and universal energy: ingredients for your miracles.

My Ignition Tip

Make the love-light that Sophia speaks of become an integral part of you, moment to moment. Live through this space and enjoy miraculous being, loving and living.

Illuminative Journalling Inquiry

What does my love-light desire me to choose?
What does my love-light require me to be?
What does my love-light require me to release?
Where does my love-light require me to go?
What does my love-light require me to do?

Spider Woman

Navajo Goddess

Dream a new world into being.

Weave your dreams into reality with love as the essence of all that you envision. Know that the best creations take great time, patience and dedication, alongside a commitment to being the best self.

Connect with your truth and know why you desire what you desire. Place love (not ego or fear) behind all your potential miracles, ensuring they arise for the highest good.

Perceive the global picture. You are here for you and at the same time, you are a citizen of humanity.

Take an even larger perspective: witness yourself through the eyes of the cosmos, see your greatness; be your greatness. The cosmos is always shifting, changing, and re-creating itself, as are we.

Know that each and every one of you co-creates your reality to varying degrees depending on your level of connection to spirit: the activation of your own wisdom and power and the amount of love you contain within and radiate outwards.

Your energetic life force when used expertly and lovingly can cause great miracles for the betterment of many.

Creation is forever in motion; connect with your own creative force.

My Ignition Tip

Surround your dreams in love for them
to become your miracles.

Illuminative Journalling Inquiry

What would I like to dream into reality, today, next
week, in the upcoming months and next year?

Thecla
Mystic

No one should dictate our lives or choices. Ignite yourself and take your life into your own hands.

Say:

I call back my power from everyone I've given it to, and from anywhere I've left it.

I call back my power from anyone or anywhere I've relinquished control at the expense of myself.

I call my power back from all times and places. I am my own.

Igniting your light and concurrent miracles is about reclaiming your power—the power that was and is always within you. Your power has been obscured from you because, throughout most of your life, you have given it away to others by making outside authority more significant and more credible than you. It is time to pull back individual power from all the people, places, times, dimensions and realities where it has been divested, both consciously and unconsciously. You are the centre of your world and when you realise this you are most effective in your world and in all of life.

All that you require to navigate this world is within you, seeded eons ago. It is time to reconnect with this power and reactivate it.

Free yourself of seeking validation and worth from others.

Free yourself of pleasing others to feel liked or valuable.

Free yourself of depending on others for wealth, status, or security of any kind.

Free yourself from forgetting that you have all the wisdom and resources within you.

Free yourself of relationships that limit you.

Free yourself of all that does not bring you joy as your power, your light, is ignited through love, peace and contentment.

Free yourself of fear because it is a power leach.

Have faith in your power and your potential to generate miracles. Your belief is your power unfolding. Believe in you: in all that you are and in all that you are becoming—immediately. Life is too precious and too powerful for you to waste another second on pretending to be all that you are not and, in doing so, playing small. Trust yourself, trust your guidance team, trust in love and in the potential beauty in all of life.

Receive all of yourself, most powerful one. Choose to be immeasurably powerful.

MY IGNITION TIP

Know who you are and allow your words and actions to reflect this. Make your life align with you at your soul level.

ILLUMINATIVE JOURNALLING INQUIRY

Say, 'Truth' before asking this question...
'Who am I?'

Thoth
Egyptian God

Dear unique sparks of the divine,

Miracles arise when a strong connection is established between heaven and Earth. Plug into your source to activate your power for miracles. Align your energy with universal energy and become a conduit for cosmic power and potential. As it is above, it must be below for true connection and unlimited possibility.

Thank you for your willingness to ignite your light and unleash your miracles. Each of you is holding within you a container of undiscovered miracles. These miracles swirl around you and within you. Respect and honour your own light and that of others to ignite your miracles. Receive your golden opportunities: your miracles.

Lift the veils of illusion that keep you trapped in your smallness.

Your power is 10.0 on the Richter scale, not -1.0. Allow the magnitude of you to be born. Allow the world to feel shockwaves of your light, love and miracles.

You are each golden arcs filled with the most diverse and one-of-a-kind treasures. Your treasure is most needed on Earth: please share this bounty for the betterment of mankind.

Learn to activate your alchemy.
- Dark into light.
- Suffering into peace.
- Fear into love.
- Despair into hope.
- Doubt into confidence.

- Judgement into compassion.
- Ego into higher self.
- Confusion into clarity.

Sharing your gifts will:
- Encourage a new way of living and being.
- Elevate technology to improve human living.
- Awaken consciousness.
- Allow healing at deep levels, purging trauma and past wounds.
- Assist others to connect with their gifts, talents and abilities.
- Encourage peace to descend, one person at a time.

Miraculous living will mean:
- Greater gifts and resources from the earth will be revealed.
- Releasing past trauma and stuck emotions to be birthed anew for meeting the new.
- Wisdom from the cosmos will be downloaded to those individuals who are ready to receive and share such transmissions.
- Accessing divine frequencies and support from the infinite cosmos for miracles.
- Opening to clairvoyance to receive inspiration and visions.
- Rising up to meet the wisdom and light of the heavens.
- Human beings will be elevated to super beings.
- Bridging the gap between heaven and Earth.
- Time will expand.
- Telepathic communication will be activated for many.

- The power of the senses will increase.
- You will experience more open communication and connection with nature.
- You can transmute lower energies from people and places that you grace with your light-filled presence.
- Food grown will reflect and resonate with what the beings around us require.
- The poisons of the earth will dissipate.
- Beauty in all things will enhance.
- The divine feminine and divine masculine will be balanced and sacred.
- Work is light. Light is work.

These are the miracles that beings of Earth require today. All I speak of is possible for all beings who seek and embrace the light. You are all chosen ones filled with golden opportunities. No being is excluded—only those who will exclude themselves via their free will beliefs, choices and actions.

MY IGNITION TIP:

Be your largeness, not your smallness.
Release yourself from the ties that bind.
Unleash all of you and awaken to the
expansive, unlimited truth of you.

ILLUMINATIVE JOURNALLING INQUIRY

How can I bridge the gap between earthly wisdom and cosmic wisdom?

Unicorns

Dear loved ones,

We see your light and receive your desire to reconnect with the magic of living. Magic has been lost on a global level from our world for some time now, but there have always been pockets of magic in existence, radiated from individuals whose magical essence burns brightly. It is time to re-ignite your magic. Your magic holds the key to your miracles. Magic does not just belong in your fairytales. Allow your living to become your own fairytale. Love your life and yourself enough to bring your fairytale to life.

Connect with the highest joy and light you have ever experienced or imagined, for that is unicorn energy. Call on us to assist you to remember this light, this energy. All of Earth needs this, even within all those people and places that reject it... for now. Bright light is catching and will reveal and illuminate shadows. Your light is most needed. Please call on us to assist with your illumination. When you speak of us, we come. Allow lightness to infuse you and your worldly concerns—we love our work with you.

Rainbow energy is akin to unicorn energy. Surround yourself with colour, with vibrancy, with possibility. Colour your world with our world. See the beauty in all of nature and within all things. Witnessing beauty in all its forms will encourage your connection with unicorn energy. Allow our world to merge with, enlighten and enliven yours. Revisit your connection with us through your childhood stories and movies and images, we have been with you for a long time... and await your new call. Your inner child will remember the way. Reconnect with him or her as a portal opening to unicorn energy. We believe it is an energy like no other and we love to share.

MY IGNITION TIP

In your meditation connect with the peace in your heart, the joy in your heart and the love in your heart to raise your frequency to best receive unicorn energy.

ILLUMINATIVE JOURNALLING INQUIRY

What would my unicorns like me to know about myself and my life this day?

Uzume
Japanese Goddess
of Laughter

Laughter, mirth, revelry, fun, play and excitement all ignite the brightest light within you, blasting away any darkness that exists in that moment. Laughter is golden. Find your humour to be miraculous. Humour elevates all those around as it is so beautifully radiant and uplifting.

Laughter is the best contagious medicine for all that ails on an emotional and physical level. Healed you is the most miraculous you. Laugh and flirt with all of life. Bring the cheeky, mischievous and loving you out to play to activate and work your light for your miracles.

Treat all of your days as days of celebration. Each morning you are still here and still breathing you get more opportunities for revelry. Build fun and play into every day as if your life depends on it—because it does. You are not truly living if you are not laughing. Your miracles require your laughter. Let go of all that stands in the way of you and your laughter. Choose to laugh today and every day thereafter.

MY IGNITION TIP

Those who make us laugh are miracles to be cherished. Surround yourself with stories, movies and people that make you laugh as often as conceivably possible.

Venusians
Star Beings

Allow your hearts and souls to travel to other worlds to reconnect with your star origins, your star purpose and your star living. Look to your stars for guidance. Open your heart and mind, stretching your capacity to receive that which has not yet been possible for you. You are all made of stardust and your stardust contains your blueprint for miracles.

Each being has their own unique core and activating this activates your miraculous life. Love yourself and all of life enough to receive all of you and your innate capabilities. Love is your portal to all of you. Your miraculous life is the one designed for you, for the highest good and is activated through consistent high-frequency functioning.

Remember who you truly are beyond your current time and space. Invite this sense of expansiveness, this sense of there being something more, into your current reality. There is more, for you are more.

Encourage your fellow man to be more. As each is more, you all become more as you are all connected. Lessen another and you lessen you. Uplift another and you uplift you. Support another and you support you. Love another and you love you. Malign another and you malign you.

You, dearest one, have a choice in who and how you will be.

Will you choose to be the you that creates miracles for all? We support you on your quest to discover all that is great and miraculous about you and your place in all of life. Enjoy the adventure of you and the pleasures within all of your life. Expand your universe to meet ours. We welcome you into a newer benevolent world. Life will manifest benevolence on Earth in response to many stepping into the best of themselves. Imagine a benevolent world. Dream it into being. What can you see? What can you create through your imagination and actions? You are more powerful as an individual and as a world than you perceive—yet.

MY IGNITION TIP

Close your eyes, relax deeply and allow your soul to envision other worlds. Travel into the stars. What can you see? Enjoy a vision journey just for you.

ILLUMINATIVE JOURNALLING INQUIRY

Record everything you saw, everything you felt and everything you learned on your star vision journey.

Wayne Dyer
Mystic

Infuse your life with spirit for it is the way to the universal and inner wisdom required for miracles. Allow divine energy to flow within you, and all around you at all times, opening you to love and its associated miracles.

Clear seeing, clarity within and awareness of all of life predisposes you to miracles. It is difficult to draw in what you don't understand. There is a system, a beautiful complexity and a divine order within miracles. The codes for you and your miracles are gently unravelled and revealed as you awaken to the truth of you and rise up to meet them. Love opens you to the plane of miracles. Conscious awareness combined with your love gifts you your miracle persona. Knowledge, love and respect for your inner landscape encompasses all you require to think, act and be the miracle worker you came here to be. Honour yourself and all of life to receive the miracle of you. Share yourself with others to help them reach a personal tipping point to access the miracle of them. Love is for sharing, replenishing and activating our best selves. Love is always the miracle.

Connect with oneness for it supports miracles of all kinds and allows transcendence over all that is in the way of your most miraculous life.

Raise your vibration to expertly hear the whispers of the universe. Embrace your guidance as miracles are co-created and seeded in spirit. Love is the way forward to meet the miracles brewing within you that can transcend current reality. Transcendence is the miracle.

Life on Earth, all of nature and all inhabitants desire

the miracle of you. Reveal and receive all of you. There is greatness within you, calling to be unleashed; it requires your surrender to love. Let love be your miraculous guide, your one true beacon of (ignited) light.

MY IGNITION TIP

Love yourself deeply to know all of you and your potential. Our miracles require the best of us.

ILLUMINATIVE JOURNALLING INQUIRY

How may I best connect with love on this day?

White Buffalo
Calf Woman,
Lakota Goddess

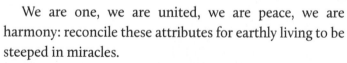

We are one, we are united, we are peace, we are harmony: reconcile these attributes for earthly living to be steeped in miracles.

Having separate containers for everything does not allow flow. Earth people must become one for peace and miracles. Miracles do not arise out of conflict, judgement, domination and fighting over resources. Miracles love peace and its high vibrational state. Miracles for changing life on Earth will arise when people on Earth change. It is a reciprocal relationship.

Earth frequency reflects the dominant energy waves emanating from the masses as a whole. Each person contributes to the energy field of Earth. Assist someone to rise up energetically and you are contributing to the elevation of the planet.

What can you do on your piece of Earth to create peace today?

- Can you express greater tolerance towards a co-worker?
- Can you love a family member more than you've been willing to before?
- Can you have gratitude for all your paid work?
- Who can you forgive?
- What personal wounds can you release and heal?
- How can you gift to nature and all her creatures in deeper ways?
- How can you serve this day?
- In what ways can you use your voice, creativity and resources to bring about positive change?

- Where in your life can you let go of all that is not in alignment with your love, soul values and purpose?

MY IGNITION TIP

Know deeply that peace contains your power
and potential and impacts the world.

ILLUMINATIVE
JOURNALLING INQUIRY

How can I become a magnet for peace
and miracles?

Yhi
Aboriginal Sun
Goddess

Allow the sun to expand your energy for receiving more light. The more light you contain, the higher your vibration becomes for generating and receiving miracles. You can draw the sun's rays into your body at any time, day or night. The sun is permanent in this world and her light is always available for those open to receiving it. Ask for sun energy to infuse your heart, mind and every cell in your body. Invite the power of the sun into your life to encourage your miracles. Feel enveloped in the white, gold, orange and yellow rays of the morning sun and allow the deeper reds of the evening sun to also flow within you and all around you. The sun's energy will activate your solar plexus and sacral chakras to invoke passion, sensuality, confidence and personal power. The sun is a universal miracle, and her energy assists you to remember that you to are a miracle capable of creating your own miracles.

Have you noticed right now on Earth that fashion features much yellow and orange? There is an awakening to the power of the sun and the healing nature of bright colours. Feel the sun, absorb the sun, and also wear the colours of the sun to lift your spirits and fill you with vitality and love for life. Love for life creates miracles. Allow the sun to inspire you and ignite your passionate nature. Honour your desire. Express your desire. Live through your desire. Be what you desire to attract what you desire.

Quench your body and soul's thirst for sunshine whenever you can. The combination of sun and nature experiences are beautifully elevating and healing. The joyful emotions activated during sunshine are great miracle inducers. Ignite your light with the greatest light of all, your sunlight.

MY IGNITION TIP:

Allow the sun to burn away darkness, revealing your most brilliant light. Feel the sun's energy filling you up from top to toe and radiating within you and all around you. Radiate this energy to every aspect of your life and to every corner of the globe.

ILLUMINATIVE JOURNALLING INQUIRY

What will my sunniest disposition create in this bright life?

MESSAGE
FOR YOU

Dear reader,

I hope you were as inspired as I was with these beautiful messages. What a gift we have been given. May these incredible 'guest contributors' inspire us to be mystics, gods and goddesses for our times.

I would love and appreciate knowing which 'mystic' resonated with you most. I am in awe of those who showed up to connect with us, to teach us, to challenge us to become the light-infused miracle workers we always knew we could be. Please reach out to me on Instagram or Facebook. I simply cannot wait to hear from you. Let me know which otherworldly being, mystic or message impacted you the most. Who spoke to your heart and soul? Who challenged you to be and receive more? Who opened something within you that had been calling for some time? Whose energy changed you on a deep level? Knowledge shared is wisdom gained and gratitude is for making miracles.

I thank you in advance for taking the time to connect with me.

LIVING A
MIRACULOUS LIFE

The beautiful thing about living a miraculous life is that each person will have their own unique experience. This is exciting because we are fuelled even more by others who are living a miracle filled-life. This energy is beautifully contagious when we exist on a similar frequency.

Living a miraculous life is a day-to-day process and journey. The wonderful thing is that miraculous living is available to us all. My miraculous life has evolved out of considerable turmoil and tests—as I'm sure yours has too. For me, learning about myself and concurrently developing a great connection with my wisdom, peace, power, love and potential arose out of some challenging states and experiences. I share this abbreviated list with you so that you can see that miracles are on the other side of our discomfort and growth; appreciate that anything is possible and a miraculous life can be just as much for you as it is for me. At any stage, after any experience, there is always the possibility of rising from the ashes into the light. We get to choose, learn, grow and choose again. That is how powerful we are.

We all have our 'list':
- Auto-immune issues
- Emotionally toxic relationships

- Navigating parenting and step-parenting
- Temporarily losing eyesight and associated trauma
- Anxiety
- Perceived entrapment and despair in career
- Lack of trust in people and in life
- Divorce
- Scarcity mentality
- Inability to truly receive
- People-pleasing
- Over-giving
- Addictive busyness
- Perfectionism
- Weak boundaries
- Fear
- Claustrophobia
- Workplace drama
- Hypersensitivity
- Not choosing for myself or receiving what would light me up

The truth is we draw these experiences to us to make us grow: to grow into our power, potential and ability to be, receive and create miracles. Nothing is random in this life; we are the co-creators of it all.

My miracle-filled life looks like this:
- Designing life as I choose it to be.
- Having a force that goes ahead of me taking care of everything in advance.
- Consistently feeling 'in love' with all of my life.
- The gift of inner peace.
- Freedom to do what I want to do when I want to do it.

- Time expands.
- New abilities and talents showing up: my writing is a miracle. I didn't know I was going to be a writer until 5 years ago. It wasn't on my radar. That is the miracle; things that were not on the radar show up seemingly out of the blue.
- Life is one big trip—adventure after adventure, new destination after new destination.
- Abundance of all kinds flows in, often in highly unexpected ways.
- Passion and purpose drive every day. This is my most-loved miracle because, in my teaching days, unease and dread were the more dominant themes. The joyful experiences were too intermingled with challenges—there was no balance.
- Life is in balance.
- Self-care opportunities abound.
- The mentors show up; the healers show up as needed.
- Nature communicates, guides and heals.
- People treat me wonderfully. Those who didn't or can't have gone away.
- Living the dream, dreaming the life.
- My husband commenting on my increasingly sparkly eyes because I'm so excited by what life presents.
- Living in the unknown world of unlimited possibility.
- Observing beauty and nature all day every day, life draws me towards beauty and adventure.
- Having gypsy freedom. I am Gypsy Jane.
- Freedom from the mundane.
- Living is ignited and inspired.

- Always creating, pioneering, leading, inventing anew.
- Re-inventing myself daily.
- Living from the heart, as the ego is sleeping or on mute.
- Living in a state of possibility.
- Connecting with higher dimensional realities and beings.
- Passion and purpose are integral in everything.
- There are no more large gaps in dreams and desires manifesting, they are often simultaneous and instantaneous.
- I am often in the right place at the right time for coincidence and synchronicity.
- The living becomes the miracle, miracles are intertwined with daily existence, they become the new normal, and not isolated surprises occurring every pancake day.
- Joy, joy, joy and more joy.
- Freedom from suffering.
- A happier, lighter body.
- Exorbitant and ongoing love and excitement for the simplest of things.
- One of my favourites is seeing a greater frequency of miracles occurring for those I love and for clients I work with. Miracles are catching!
- Life pivots in unexpected, amazing ways. I can be cruising along happily with my path and then 'wow', a new unforeseen trajectory, pathway or opportunity arises.
- Gratitude infuses all moments and experiences.
- I have a get-up-and-go attitude: where to next?

- With my gypsy freedom, I can work from anywhere.
- I am showing up for the work, and the work is showing up for me.
- Time power: I wrote over half of this book in a month! My first book took over 3 years.
- I've published 3 books in 3 years. My 'trilogy' is complete.

What does a miracle-filled life look like for you?

The key to creating a miracle-filled life is unashamedly and unreservedly claiming, owning, and acknowledging all our great magic and miracles. It requires not lessening our miracles or making them smaller to make others feel better or less inadequate. It is allowing others to rise up to meet you, whereas previously you may have diminished yourself to fit in. It means no longer hiding our miracles or the truth of our miracle personas. It is now embracing, 'look at me and what I can do'. This is not from a place of ego but from excitement for life, gratitude, celebration and acknowledgement of infinite potential. It's about releasing the superhuman within us all that desires to be free and expressing this fully. Love your life (starting with what is presenting) and love your miracles into existence.

PART 3

EMERGING ABILITIES

So, what are we really capable of?
What abilities may be emerging within us?

The amazing consequence of igniting our light is that our miracle personas are unleashed within. From here, we enjoy a flow on of magical occurrences in our external world. As we step up into our true potential, some truly extraordinary abilities may emerge. We are brave pioneers travelling into unknown waters with an open heart and faith in the perhaps (previously determined) 'impossible' elements of life. Abilities that we have witnessed only in movies may potentially become part of our new reality. I believe that all abilities that are 'bestowed' on us are gifted only to those enlightened enough to use their gifts for the highest good; for healing, transforming and elevating others. Belief is everything in creating these new abilities. For me, there are more questions than knowledge and answers. However, I know in every part of my body and soul that anything is possible if we can imagine it first. We dreamed of flying and the aeroplane was created. What if we all dreamed that we could actually fly? Many believe the power of combined intention knows no parallels.

Various individuals seem to have greater proclivities towards different abilities. What captivates you is perhaps an indication of where your unique talents originate.

In the upcoming pages are some possible gifts that have crossed my awareness: my knowledge being limited and only through the lens of my understanding. Feel free to carry out your own research and tap into the knowledge of any individuals who may be breaking new ground in this area. What follows is a snapshot of what may be possible.

Alchemy

Alchemy involves transforming one condition into something greater.

In ancient times alchemy was associated with material transformation, changing water into wine and base metal into gold: creating transformation via changing energy states. During these times, alchemy was also associated with mystical transformation to the highest levels of human potential.

Changing the ordinary into the extraordinary is alchemy in action. We are already being alchemists every time we transmute fear and all its derivatives into love; free our energy to effect change; transform problems into solutions; and release old patterns and create new living.

Become your own alchemist, changing perceived problems or personal limitations into something greater, bringing forth powerful change. Alchemy is about using our energy wisely, channelling it to where it is most needed and most effective at any given time. It is understanding that alchemy is a precious resource for creating our lives. Alchemy also involves mystical transformation as we cannot always see the changes that are emerging through us and for us as we connect with unlimited universal energies.

Dr Joe Dispenza teaches that a powerful way to access our ability to alchemize is through breath work, calming our nervous system to the place where we switch from our sympathetic nervous system to our parasympathetic nervous system. Dr Joe believes this prepares the body to move into a creative state and into the field of infinite potential.

The best alchemists allow energy to move through them, they transmute it into something greater. Alchemists don't allow inner storms to settle in, they feel them, release them and receive the underlying wisdom. Alchemists trust they are always connected to love; guidance and insight are always available, and that miracles are always possible. Alchemists listen more to the voice of love as opposed to the voice of fear. Experiencing fear and all its derivatives is uncomfortable and serves the purpose of increasing our commitment to alchemising fear into love. Alchemists recognise that their intuitive powers are an integral aspect of miracles: knowing when to listen and act on the inner wisdom providing the bread crumb trail to miracles. Over time, through honouring and accepting the intuitive process without resistance, we step into our true alchemy.

We appreciate that the contrasting states we feel help to move us forward. Sometimes to know what we desire we need to experience the opposite—providing fuel for moving forward. It becomes a natural part of how we navigate life. We value ourselves, knowing we deserve miracles. Peace and miracles are ours once we have alchemised all that is in the way of experiencing it.

Personal expansion through our alchemy exponentially increases our potential for creating and drawing in miracles. We become living miracles as we can now access our full repertoire of gifts, talents and abilities. This is who we are once we have alchemised our way to true inner freedom and our greatest potential as creative beings.

Animal Communication

Imagine a world where we were all animal whisperers. It requires much expansive thinking to even be able to envisage what we could learn from the animal kingdom. Our connection to nature would advance astronomically with greater communion with all the creatures of Earth.

The benefits of being able to connect with the true needs and messages of animals would be immeasurable. We would aspire to establish more successful co-habitation on Earth. There is (at this stage) inconceivable potential for working together to create life-enhancing outcomes for both humankind and animals. Enhanced animal communication would mean so much uplevelling in terms of care and healing for animals in both reserves and the wild. The threat of extinction for many species would be reduced or even eradicated.

What we learn from animals and experience whilst in their presence is already truly amazing, just imagine a deeper connection.

Changing Energies & Atmosphere

The more light we hold within, the greater the light that radiates from us out into the world. As we step into our miracle personas, our mere presence is enough to change the energy in another, in a room and even on a much larger scale. I have certainly experienced the change in the mood and vision of individuals after being in my presence as I know you have too. I have witnessed being in the presence of a powerful, radiant being and felt the energy shift in all those around me. Never underestimate your ability to transmute lower energies within those that you encounter. Be the gift for others that you truly are.

Imagine millions of people all over the planet lit up within, embracing the full power and spectrum of their light. Whole areas, even towns and countries could change and evolve in ways beyond what we have ever seen.

✦
The Clairs

Clairvoyance involves the gift of clear seeing. It may involve seeing flashes of light in the peripheral vision, references to the future, visions, colour, images, scenes and symbols. Individuals can then decode the messages within the imagery with increasing skill. Often the symbolism will be followed by words or even another image until the message is received. The images are often delivered through our own frame of reference. Developing clairvoyance may begin by receiving visual signs in the physical world first and then seeing with the third eye.

Clairaudience involves hearing messages and sounds in both the physical world and in the inner ear. There may be repetitive thoughts, songs and lyrics used to create meaning.

Clairsentience involves feeling and sensing what another is experiencing. It can involve changes in bodily sensation, temperature, pressure, mood and energy.

Clairalience involves receiving messages through smell that is reminiscent of people, situations and places.

Clairgustance connects individuals with taste as a way of triggering memory and receiving a message, often with the experience of metallic, sour, sweet or spicy tastes.

Claircognizance is a strong knowledge of what is occurring within us, for others and in situations. There can be a clear understanding of what has happened or is going to happen.

Cloaking

Have you ever had the experience of feeling like you are completely invisible (from a physical standpoint) to others? I feel like many of us already raise our vibration and expand our energy in some way to be more infinite than finite. This perhaps has the effect of those around us (maybe those vibrating at a lower frequency) not noticing our presence. Imagine the potential for only being seen if we wanted to be seen. It sounds like a very peace-inducing ability to me.

Communion with Technology

Like me, you have probably witnessed the correlation between an idea, a desire or a fantasy becoming a reality through the arrival of corresponding technology. Someone somewhere knows how to create anything that can be imagined. We are most certainly already seeing this ability show up on our planet. It may take time, but it is happening. Something new has been invented to match the 'dream'. Throughout history, any innovation has arisen out of an individual (or the power of many) imagining such a possibility. Technology matches both desires and needs. The potential for new technology is therefore beyond this world! What technology can we imagine into being for the betterment of mankind? I'd like a body scanner to tell me exactly what my body requires and desires for optimal health and wellbeing and a device to heal anything that requires healing before disease can set in. Imagine being able to apply this technology to animals and individuals who don't have a 'voice.' I would also love a device to record the designs and images I create within my mind onto paper or a screen.

What can you imagine into reality to enhance life for us all?

Expanding Time

The first half of this book took around 6 months to write. At the halfway point I received very clear guidance and the urge to complete the book in a month... for it desired to be out in the world. The 'smaller' part of me felt the impossibility of this scenario however the expansive (miracle persona) version of me knew that somehow, someway it would happen. I trusted that life and time would conspire to support this eventuality. I initially felt that it might require much 'leaving' my life in the form of clients, social engagements and other 'adventures'. Miraculously, this was not the case. In fact, my life moved into perfect balance: time expanded; more opportunities for writing arose; 1 was able to schedule all clients, and self-care flowed effortlessly within my days to fully support me and the work. The whole scenario showed me what is possible—more so than 1 had previously imagined—when we step into our miraculous selves.

Belief and trust in our miracle selves and simultaneously in the power of the universe are of paramount importance in creating expanded time. Ask regularly, 'How can time expand for me in this situation?' Enjoy what occurs.

Finding Things
That Are Lost

Have you ever had the experience of losing a treasured possession or even just something useful like one's keys and then having them re-appear in places that they were not previously? You know said object wasn't there as you had already looked in that place several times. 1 believe demand and intent has its own inherent power behind miracles. The mere desire to have an object come back to us may in fact cause miracles. Perhaps we are changing the molecular structure of something for it to move through time and space or simply translocating it with our energy as the impetus? Whatever the case, 1 find this to be a very mysterious and frequently occurring phenomenon.

Healing With Energy

There is much occurring in the world around the potential of energy healing for healing ourselves and others. Energy healing is concerned with establishing balance and flow within the body: addressing and clearing emotional, mental and spiritual issues that may be interfering with this flow and creating disease. Reiki, acupuncture, pranic healing, sound healing, yoga, crystal healing, sound therapy, chanting, kinesiology, quantum healing, qigong and emotional freedom technique (tapping) are currently very popular and highly successful modalities.

As we align with the heavens and connect with Earth, we prime ourselves to be conduits for healing energy: able to channel this energy into our bodies and into those of others for healing and transformation. We are energetic beings and energy is our true language. Energy will always be a greater guide than words when seeking truth. Taking care of our energetic chakra system is essential for maximum health and wellbeing. Just as bodily systems like the circulatory, digestive and endocrine systems underpin our health, so too does our energetic system. We invoke miracles when we take care of our energetic bodies. We become present, aware, mindful, and more peaceful and loving as we connect with our true essence. Our mental and emotional wellbeing, our vitality and immunity are enhanced. Energy healing is so effective as it takes care of things that are arising in our energetic field before they can make their way into our emotional, mental, and physical bodies causing dis-ease and then disease. Many believe that disease does not shift from the body until the underlying emotional contributors are addressed. Much illness stays in the body as people are unable to change the mind stories that play on repeat daily. Energy healing has a miraculous way of being able to bypass the mind and heal from the inside out, calming and clearing the mind and shifting from the body unprocessed toxic emotions at the same time. Energy healing is a miracle for all to share and access. It will most certainly help to ignite your most powerful light.

Heightened Senses

I wonder as we continue to claim our super potential what may be possible for our senses. I imagine our senses will develop far beyond what is currently in existence within us. Will our eyesight improve, perhaps seeing over greater distances or more clearly in the dark? Will our hearing, taste and smell develop? Will more individuals become empaths—feeling what those around them are experiencing? Empaths feel and respond to the energy an individual or a situation is emitting more than the words that are spoken as the greater truths are contained within the energy. If there is dissonance between the two forms of communication, it can be extremely uncomfortable for empaths. Perhaps in our new world there will be more authentic communication with people saying and vibrating their truth out into the world.

Perhaps, our sixth sense, our psychic gifts may become even stronger. There may even be other senses that have not appeared within humans yet. When we rise up even more, claiming our super selves, there may be corresponding advances in all our forms of perception. Our ability to process our world may develop greatly and in previously unexperienced ways. I imagine there is much within us that is currently dormant, waiting for us to rise to meet it. What is truly possible for us? What do you perceive emerging within us, for us?

✦

Influencing the Weather

I am wondering if you may have had the experience of affecting the weather. I have played with asking the clouds to part and letting the sunshine through and asking for no rain as I am walking from one place to another. It is uncanny how many times the weather changes upon request. Could this be a lucky coincidence, or something more miraculous occurring within us and around us? Often the weather changes are only momentary... could this be determined by our belief in miracles? I imagine nature is always in charge and we receive little gifts (miracles) of weather changes in our location.

✦

Manifestation

Manifestation is certainly a prominent word in our current spiritual culture. I believe that as we step more fully into our light and the energy of our miracles our manifestation power will proliferate. Boom! What we desire and require shows up in record time. Rather than our manifestation process taking years, it may only take weeks, days, or a moment in time. The distance between dream and reality will be reduced, making us even more aware of how our energy and beliefs magnetise our miracles towards us. Remember raising our vibration is integral to enhanced manifestation abilities.

✴

Meeting Our Spirit Guides

I have already mentioned previously the magic and power associated with connecting with our spiritual guidance team. Over time I see this becoming more commonplace, not something us weird (aware) spiritual types do. Connecting with guides, angels, masters, mystics, ancestors, gods, goddesses and otherworldly beings may become the new norm in an ever-increasing advanced society.

Meditation is the key to connecting with the guidance available from other dimensions—we have to learn a new way of listening. The more we 'listen' the more we can connect. Quieting the day-to-day busy mind is paramount. Remember the voice (heard in your voice) of guidance is always positive: encouraging you to feel grounded, loved and safe. There will be no outcome agenda within this guidance, and it won't be forceful or drama-filled as the ego voice may often be.

Phasing

Phasing is something we witness in movies where beings can change their energy to the point of being able to move through objects rather than going around them. I feel that ideas in fantasy books and movies have a level of potential truth and possibility contained within, such is my openness to all things.

Perhaps fantastical abilities we see within X-Men and Marvel movies and the like are revealing to us or teasing us with some potential possible abilities in the future human race. The seeds of new abilities may be actually sown in imaginative books and movies. There is nothing more wonderful than merging into fantasy worlds. Perhaps one day fantasy may merge with reality. Stay open.

Probability Manipulation

The experience of changing the probability of something occurring is very mysterious and magical. It seems to arise out of an intense momentary demand where we suspend time to be able to avoid or move out of the way of something that is perhaps dangerous or drama-inducing. Averting danger or avoiding life-threatening circumstances creates a 'pressure' within us that creates miracles, just as coal under pressure creates diamonds. In an instant, we defy the ego and its reality-defining aspect of our being and step into our super selves. Like me, you have probably heard stories of mothers who perform super acts to protect children or individuals that fall from buildings and remain miraculously and mind-defyingly unhurt.

For me, this phenomenon has shown up when I have somehow moved into position to catch something before it breaks or miraculously avoided a fall after tripping.

I certainly had this experience with my 'non-car accident' several years ago. I pulled out of a side street and didn't see a car pulling out of a driveway. We collided, and I felt the impact, as did the people in the other car because they had very angry faces. When we got out of our respective cars to inspect the damage, the cars were not touching and there was no damage. The people in the other car drove away stunned and speechless and I knew something miraculous had transpired. Somehow time and space had shifted and 'probability' was most certainly challenged.

✦
Prophetic &
Healing Dreams

I have healing dreams quite regularly, showing up in a myriad of ways. Most common and most miraculous is extreme, out-of-this-world orgasmic energy flowing through my body. This often occurs during nights when I go to bed with aches and pains, feeling unwell or after being around strong energies that are still impacting me prior to sleep. It also occurs every time I uplevel in some way, transitioning from an old way of being and functioning into the new. The butterfly obviously needs some kind of push to leave her cocoon. I've also experienced strange vortexes of energy that feel like I'm dropping into a new space. This sensation is often accompanied by new insight and revelations.

Often, I will dream of people that I am going to meet with in the future or of people from my past that I need to reconnect with. Guidance comes to us in so many ways through our dreams. Stay open and receptive to all that may be possible for you in the land of your very own dreams. I believe our dreamscape is an untapped opportunity for creating miracles within us and in our lives. Lucid dreaming (knowing you are dreaming whilst dreaming) teaches us how to create anything we desire. Lucid dreams feel like I'm overseeing all of creation when whatever I choose to create in that moment shows up on the canvas of my current dream. Perhaps this is the potential and possibility we are being shown for creating our own 'dream' reality in our daily living. I have often attempted to bring this creative energy back into my waking hours to connect more fully with miracle me.

I also revisit beautiful loving moments, as far back as my childhood during sleep. The elevated feelings fuel my days and are such a simple way to raise our vibration to attract miracles.

Stars are one of the symbols my guidance team place in my path to show me when I am on track. One night I dreamt vividly of a silver star necklace that my grade 6 boyfriend gave me (thank you SW), and I know it was my guides showing up for me through a very poignant and loving moment. I felt cherished and these feelings stayed with me all day. I've also asked that this necklace make its way back to me in some way and I am eagerly awaiting this miracle, I know it's already on its way.

Many of us connect with our magic and miracles by visiting the astral plane and also potentially other times, dimensions and worlds. Be open to the portal to your potential within your dreams. If you can dream it, you can create it.

Allow your dream world to infuse your real world with magic and miracles.

Before going to sleep, be quiet and calm. Ask your guidance team to connect you with the possibilities for more of your potential to open that is contained within your dreams. Set the intent to remember your dreams and to experience lucid dreaming.

Ask, 'What message and potential for unlocking the miracle of me can be revealed through last night's dreams?' I remember one night before going to sleep I had asked for a clue as to how well my books would be received. Very loudly (so much so that it woke me up with a start) I heard, 'Success is imminent'. This was such a beautiful gift and I have carried that belief and energy within me ever since.

Psychometry

Psychometry involves sensing information about people, places, and events by holding objects and is therefore often known as object reading. Through the objects people see and sense things that are not normally perceived. Every object, living or non-living, has an energy and contains information for us if we are open to receiving it. Through a piece of clothing or jewellery, we are often able to sense a lot about a person, perhaps even future events that may be unfolding for them. Clothing and jewellery also contain memories associated with events that can solidify in our psyche. That is why it is so beneficial to de-clutter and release items we possess that don't make us feel good.

We can also sense the past via touch. Some individuals particularly adept at this practice hold the object in their hands or to the forehead (third eye), stilling the mind and connecting with the object. This process most likely uses our 'clair' gifts.

Impressions can be perceived as images, sounds, smells, tastes and even emotions. All objects store energy and this can influence what things we enjoy or don't enjoy having in our space. I have never felt truly peaceful being in old homes containing lots of antiques: there is just too much of the past contained within much of the furniture and artifacts that it can be a little overwhelming. The old saying, 'the walls have ears' is particularly relevant in this case, but I think objects have ears too!

Emotions and vibrations are strongly imbued in an object. We often witness the power and energy of objects with individuals who give away gifts that are associated with painful memories. This is often because the energy contained within the object triggers old memories, making it more difficult to move forward.

When developing object reading skills, practise makes imperfectly perfect. Calm and still the mind. Close your eyes and tune into an object of your choice and see what is revealed to you.

✦

Raising Our Collective Vibration

Raising our vibration is not only conducive to feeling great and manifesting miracles on a personal level. It can also be a miraculous phenomenon when occurring simultaneously in large groups of individuals within proximity to each other. The infinite potential of coming together (as a large collective) for a common higher purpose is quite mind-boggling. Some ancient civilisations that are believed to have just 'disappeared' from our planet have theories surrounding them implying that these groups of people raised their frequency so high, enabling entry into other dimensions.

Remote Viewing

Remote viewing is concerned with being able to see beyond our current location. Imagine a looking-glass swirling with various scenes from other times or places: a crystal ball-type effect of seeing into the future or back into the past.

Energetically we may be open to observing and perceiving outside our current senses. It may involve reaching out to connect with the universal collective consciousness to enter new spaces. This may have the potential for advanced use of consciousness to investigate other times, places, spaces, and dimensions beyond our current place in time to enhance our current functioning on Earth.

Superpower

In our world, there are some phenomenal healing modalities and advances in science and medicine to prolong our years. As we grow in consciousness and begin to heal as a species, I wonder what is possible for us within our evolution. I perceive we will become more intelligent, more intuitive and more psychic. I wonder what increasing consciousness could mean for our bodily capacities. Could we develop super strength, speed and other abilities that we have only had exposure to in movies?

Telekinesis

Telekinesis involves moving objects with the mind. It is using the power of our thoughts and energy to manipulate the location of objects. It may involve being able to open and shut doors, turn off light switches or swing a pendulum as many of us have seen 'demonstrated' in movies. I imagine this super trait could make us quite lazy but there is a time, place and benefit for all manner of things under the sun.

Telepathy

Telepathy is the transmission of information via thought from one person to another without any physical interaction. Many of us have experienced 'hearing' the thoughts of another: a person says something we were only moments away from speaking. This most often occurs when we have a very close connection with another individual. We tune into their essence and being on a higher level.

Telepathy occurs most successfully with intent, calming breath and a very still mind. Clearing our higher chakras may also assist telepathic communication as we are creating a clearer channel for transmission.

You may wish to test your telepathic capacities by expanding your energy outwards to connect with another person. Focus your attention on the person you want to communicate with, visualise them, think of them, surround them in loving light. If you know a person well there may be more chance of connecting with them as they may potentially be open to receiving you and your energetic communication. If an individual is attempting to send you telepathic communication, you may start thinking about them. Many of us have had the experience of thinking about someone moments before they call us. Try it with a friend. Repeat a loving message over and over and see if they can receive it. Success is most likely influenced by your own mind control and belief in the process.

Telepathy indicates there is more connectedness between us than we currently perceive. Moving from separateness to wholeness connects us with our innate peace, contentment, gifts and miraculous predispositions and abilities, perhaps more than we realise.

Translocation

I perceive that much of our newer emerging abilities will come into being when we as a species uplevel enough to receive them and to utilise them for the highest good. What may once have been science fiction may become reality.

Translocation is one such ability that creates awe in moviegoers: being able to move from one location to another.

If I use my imagination, I 'see' with translocation that if we reach advanced stages of consciousness and can connect deeply with love, we can move through a portal within our heart, envisioning where we choose to be and moving our energy to that space. I'm seeing us being able to visit these places energetically but not taking our actual physical bodies along for the ride. Perhaps my version is extremely limited. What do you see as a possibility?

Somewhere we have been taught that as adults there is a wrongness in imagining and believing in what has been considered impossible, perhaps risking being labelled as too weird or too different. The world needs us to embrace the full spectrum of our weirdness to move beyond the mundane and into the realm of miracles. Be open to all that is outside your current senses and push past your limits beyond that part of you that has decided that anything is 'far-fetched and impossible'. Perhaps consider that much of what we thought was real and true may not be... sometimes there is truth in the very opposite of what we have known.

The secret to much of our power and abilities is contained within our hearts. Open to more of yourself to open to your true potential and emerging abilities. Our hearts connect us with our souls and create a beautiful bridge between heaven and Earth.

I see us all with golden keys: at last, turning them to open to the unknown mysteries and potential within us and, in doing so, opening to the infinite wonder in the world and the universe. Trust in the wonder, magic, miracles and emerging abilities that are revealing themselves to you, for you.

Meet your gifts, talents and abilities and share them with others. Gifts are for sharing and your gifts can change the world.

Miracle Persona

Just for you, here is a summary of your new miracle-inducing persona. As you have come to realise, becoming a miracle worker is about stepping into the truth, the power and the greatest potential of you. This is your natural state, the meeting of the real you, the person you rediscover after all that was obscuring 'super you' (from you) has been shifted. You are brand new with a clean slate to generate miracles.

Feel miraculous.
Live from the space of all experiences having silver linings to encourage relishing all of life rather than resisting it.
Angle your life towards positive experiences.
Be extremely grateful for everything that shows up in your life.
Free yourself from self-sabotage.
See the wonder in both the extraordinary and the ordinary.
Free yourself from limiting beliefs.
Go within to free yourself and heal yourself.
Listen to the wisdom of your body.
Balance giving and receiving to be your most powerful.
Know yourself and your motivations.
Love yourself and all of life.
Indulge in relentless self-care to feel and be your best.
Unblock beliefs impacting your abundance.
Love your work.

Be present to maximise your peace and power.

Stop caring about anything that limits you; focus your attention and energy on your potential miracles.

Be vigilant with the management of your mind.

Re-direct all harmful thinking to positive alternatives.

Uplevel your beliefs so they are aligned with your highest good and true desires.

Keep your energies clear and your boundaries strong, that is, be very clear about what you will and will not accept from yourself and others.

Access your inner wisdom and intuitive powers.

Listen to your own inner voice so you can entrain yourself to hear the wisdom of your guides.

Live as peace, love, and flow.

Be a pleasure seeker as you are in fact inadvertently seeking miracles simultaneously.

Elevate your emotions and therefore your vibration to draw in great experiences.

Act on intuitive hunches for they are your miracle markers.

Read inspiring and uplifting literature. Awareness is peace, power and worth.

Treat your worth like the most precious of heirlooms.

Keep the miracle blockers (worry, doubt, fear, comparison, envy, negative thinking and anxiety) at bay.

Flow and surrender. You don't want to 'control' miracles as they originate from the infinite unknown.

Anticipate the best.

Be optimistic.

Be joy.

AFTERWORD

Thank you for opening to your own miracle persona and thus being such a bright light in our world. Enjoy your ignited light. May these words be your new way of living: 'I open to more, I open to more of me and to more of life.' Allow this work to lead you down a path for connecting with something greater: something greater within you, within life and within the infinite universe. The magical, mystical place within us, that is calling for us, is where our miracles live. Enjoy expanding your very outer limits of what is possible, going where few have ventured before.

Miracles of all manner of magnitude begin with us. Every person that changes contributes to change in the world. You have changed via the words and energy within these pages, and you will create ripple effects with your miraculous presence. Millions of individuals all activating their miracle personas can invoke global and cosmic change. That is the power of us. The miracles we experience in our lifetime are representative of the collective. We are all responsible for elevating consciousness to enjoy the infinite spectrum of miracles. Rising together will allow us to reach new heights.

The miracles we desire are on the other side of our combined love, awareness, creativity, vision, power and most radiant light—all arising from within us. Thank you for your part in dreaming, imagining and weaving our new world into being. May your miracles evolve as you evolve...

into the truly spectacular.

Belief determines whether our miracles involve flying on the dragon's back or observing from the ground while someone else soars off into the clouds. Appreciating all miracles builds their momentum and magnitude. We need to be willing to 'see' the miracle in what we may have deemed 'ordinary' before we can turn ice into fire, water into wine or lead into gold.

After taking this journey with me you will come to know that our miracles are drawn to the best of us. However, there are always paradoxes in life and life often does what life does, on its own terms. Accept all that life offers as a potential miracle. Keep the faith, keep hope alive, for miracles can arrive at any moment because they are as the name suggests: miracles. Changing the focus on what is wrong in our lives to what is very right, switching and resetting from expecting the worst to anticipating the best, allows magic, miracles and synchronicity to enter.

There is never one set formula for our miracles as everyone has their own unique blueprint for creating and receiving miracles. Sometimes our miracles are called forth when we are under great pressure as we make a subconscious demand on ourselves to be more and receive more than we've ever been willing or able to previously. Pressure can rocket us into the space of miracles and force us to claim our miracle personas out of deep necessity.

Miracles are always unexpected surprises; believe that they can arrive for you at any moment just by being your beautiful self. You are always enough for your miracles. Miracles are our divine birthright even on days we are not feeling so divine. All the good you feel and create on any day goes into your miracle bank, so there is always plenty of firepower in reserve to fuel your low vibe days. Always keep close to your heart that you are the miracle you have been waiting for, and now that you've arrived, look out world!

Be the miracle worker that you came here to be.
We are light ignited and miracles unleashed.
We have ignition.

Yours, in anticipation of your miracles,
Jane

ACKNOWLEDGEMENTS

Thank you to all the magical, wise beings from all times, spaces and worlds who have contributed to assisting us to ignite our light and unleash our miracles.

We now have the best possible chance of unlocking our personal blueprint for miracles. We can be of this world and out of this world simultaneously. What a gift this is.

I feel honoured to be the messenger for your much-needed voices. This experience has been life-changing. I have connected even more fully with the knowledge that the energy of a person is infinite, eternal, and forever evolving and shaping the entire universe. We are that powerful, that miraculous.

Natasha Gilmour, Publisher at the kind press, thank you for believing in the work of an unknown author from Tasmania. I am ever so grateful that my work was resonant with the philosophy of your beautiful kind press. The whole process from creation to publication has been light ignited, miracles unleashed.

Don, thanks for being you and for helping me to see miracles and to use imagination, hope and joy for creating them.

ABOUT THE
AUTHOR

Jane Holman conducts energy healing, intuitive counselling and life coaching through her business, Reiki One, whilst providing considerate direction and genuine motivation for aspiring writers.

Her third book, *Light Ignited, Miracles Unleashed: A Cosmic Blueprint for Your Miracles* flows gracefully and powerfully from her previous two books *Seeds of Self-Care: For Love and Serenity* and *Pearls of Wisdom: For Your Path to Peace.*

A GIFT FROM THE AUTHOR

Visit janeholman.com.au to receive a **Free Wallpaper Download** as a daily reminder to connect with your heart space to *ignite your light, unleash your miracles* and open up to your cosmic potential as a mystical magical being.

'Anchor into the power, love and serenity of yourself and we will take you beyond the rainbow.'

– My Spiritual Guidance Team

CPSIA information can be obtained
at www.ICGtesting.com
Printed in the USA
LVHW050411081122
732583LV00004B/22